MY BROTHER'S FACE

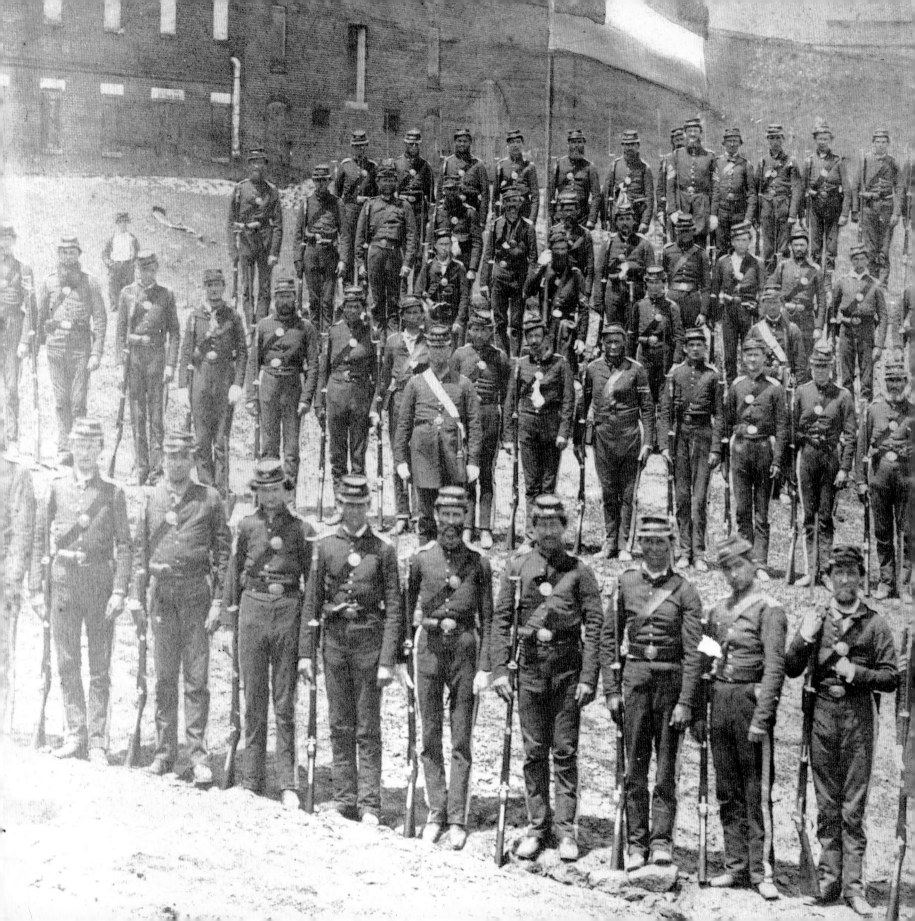

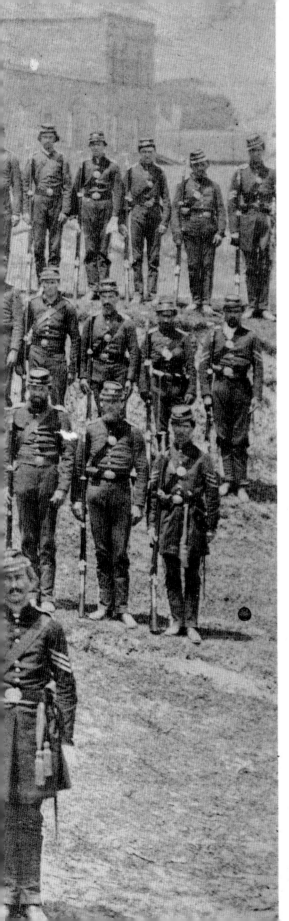

MY BROTHER'S FACE

PORTRAITS OF THE CIVIL WAR
IN PHOTOGRAPHS, DIARIES, AND LETTERS

BY

CHARLES PHILLIPS AND ALAN AXELROD

FOREWORD BY

BRIAN C. POHANKA

Chronicle Books • San Francisco

Printed in Hong Kong.

Library of Congress Cataloging-in-Publication Data

Phillips, Charles, 1948-
    My brother's face: portraits of the Civil War in photographs, diaries, and letters /
        by Charles Phillips and Alan Axelrod; foreword by Brian C. Pohanka.
        p. cm.
    Includes bibliographical references and index.
    ISBN 0-8118-0162-4
    1. United States—History—Civil War, 1861-1865—Campaigns.
    2. United States—History—Civil War, 1861-1865—Campaigns—
    Pictorial works. I. Axelrod, Alan, 1952- . II. Title.
    E470.P44   1993
    973.7'3—dc20   92-13958
                                        CIP

Book design by Zenda, Inc.
Photo research: Curtis A. Utz
Picture credits: *Library of Congress:* frontispiece, 5, 8, 10, 11, 17, 21, 25, 26, 29, 33, 35, 38, 39, 40–41, 42, 45, 51, 53, 55, 58–59, 61, 63, 67, 68–69, 71, 76–77, 79, 82, 84, 87, 88–89, 95, 97, 106, 109, 110, 117, 126–27, 129, 131, 132, 138–39, 140, 143, 144, 147

U. S. Army Military History Institute: 12–13, 18, 22–23, 30–31, 36–37, 64–65, 72, 80–81, 91, 99, 103, 105, 114–15, 119, 121, 122, 125, 135

National Archives: 14, 47, 48–49, 57, 66, 75, 83, 92, 113, 136, 148
The quotation on page 79 is reproduced from the *Diary of Colonel William Lamb* in the Earl Gregg Swem Library, College of William and Mary. The quotations on page 107 and page 108 are reproduced from *The Civil War Notebook of Daniel Chisholm,* edited by W. Springer Menge and J. August Shimrak, published by Ballantine Books, 1990. The quotation on page 117 is from page 51 of *A Woman Doctor's Civil War: Esther Hill Hawk's Diary,* edited by Gerald Schwartz, published by University of South Carolina Press, 1984, 1989 (reprinted by permission, 1992).

Distributed in Canada by Raincoast Books, 112 East Third Ave.,
Vancouver, B.C. V5T 1 C8

C.1

10 9 8 7 6 5 4 3 2 1

Chronicle Books
275 Fifth Street
San Francisco, CA 94103

CONTENTS

PHOTOGRAPHING THEIR BROTHER'S FACE

by Brian C. Pohanka

On October 29, 1863, the soldiers of the 19th Connecticut Volunteer Infantry had just completed their daily ritual of drill and dress parade near their camp at Alexandria, Virginia, when twenty-one-year-old Private Lewis Bissell discovered that his unit would have an additional duty to perform. "When we had formed in line a daguerrian artist came on the ground to take our 'mugs,'" the private noted in a letter to his family. "He took us standing in line of battle, in four ranks, in a hollow square and in four ranks at bayonet charge."

While the identity of Bissell's "daguerrian artist" is lost to history, it is unlikely that any of the New Englanders would have been surprised by his presence. By the 1860s, photography had become a fact of life for most Americans, and theirs was a much-photographed war.

Photography was halfway through its fourth decade when the long-simmering tensions between North and South erupted in conflict. The earliest permanent photographic image had been made in 1826 by the Frenchman Joseph Niepce: a blurry view of rooftops and chimneys that had required an eight-hour exposure. Three years later Niepce joined forces with Louis Jacques Mande Daguerre, an enterprising artist and technical innovator who developed and marketed the first reliable photographic technique. Initially publicized in 1839, the daguerrean process recorded remarkably clear images on copper sheets plated with polished silver. By the late 1840s, hundreds of daguerreotypists were operating in the United States, among them the painter and telegraph inventor Samuel F. B. Morse and a young New York entrepreneur named Mathew Brady.

The fledgling photographic art took another dramatic step forward in 1851 when Englishman Frederick Scott Archer announced his invention of a process that enabled photographic images to be recorded on plates of glass coated with a chemical called collodion. After preparation in the darkroom, a wet collodion plate was carried to the camera in a light-proof holder. The photographer exposed the plate by uncapping the camera lens for an average of fifteen to thirty seconds, depending on the available light, then carried the plate back to the darkroom for developing and fixing in a series of chemical solutions.

Taking advantage of Archer's collodion process, Bostonian James A. Cutting patented the ambrotype in 1854: collodion glass negatives, which, when backed with black paper, varnish, or metal, were transformed into positive images. Ambrotypes soon supplanted daguerreotypes in popularity, since they could be viewed more easily; daguerreotypes had to be tilted at just the right angle in order to make a clear positive image visible. Yet another variation—the ferrotype or tintype—recorded images on sheets of iron that had been coated with a light-sensitive emulsion.

Ambrotypes and tintypes, like the earlier daguerreotypes, could not be reproduced. In that sentimental Victorian age, these one-of-a-kind images of loved ones were treated as revered icons. Photographic enthusiast Dr. Oliver Wendell Holmes described them as "faithful memorials of those whom we love and would remember."

Daguerreotypes and ambrotypes were invariably mounted in decorative velvet-lined gutta-percha cases, while tintypes were often set into lockets or pocket watches. All three of these direct-image techniques recorded a mirror image of the sitter or scene; during the Civil War it was not uncommon for soldiers to compensate for this distortion by reversing their weapons and accoutrements, while photographers sometimes used paint to "touch out" the backward letters on buttons and military beltplates.

The collodion process permitted photographers one other alternative, which by the late 1850s had supplanted all others in the public's love affair with the camera. From glass negatives, contact prints could be made on paper that had been coated with albumen—a mixture of egg whites, salt, and ammonium chloride. Albumen prints were neither reversed nor unique; indeed, a potentially limitless number of prints could be made from a single negative. Their marketability proved an economic bonanza for photographic galleries, particularly in the 2 1/2 x 4-inch *carte-de-visite* format, which enabled common citizens to augment their family picture albums with images of royalty, celebrities, and military commanders. The trading and collecting of these pictorial visiting cards inspired Dr. Holmes to dub them "the social currency, the sentimental 'greenbacks' of civilization."

While the American Civil War was not the first conflict to be recorded by the camera—an anonymous daguerreotypist

had made at least a dozen views during the Mexican War, and British photographer Roger Fenton had taken 360 glass plate images in the Crimean conflict of 1854-55—the struggle between the Union and Confederacy was without precedent in the nature and extent of its photographic coverage.

With some 4,000 American photographers at work by 1861, it became an almost ritual procedure for enthusiastic and untried volunteers to record their warlike mien for friends and family. Heads clamped firmly in the inevitable supporting rod that prevented blurring during the long exposure time, they did their best to appear heroic, if more than a little stiff and self-conscious. Since soldiers were generally forbidden to carry muskets or sidearms into town, the weapons they held were often studio props rather than regulation firearms. The photographer's set was frequently enhanced by such artificial trappings as Grecian pillars, brocaded curtains, and painted backdrops, which combined classical themes with Victorian parlor decor—an incongruous setting for fearsome warriors.

Whenever a lull in campaigning allowed, Yanks and Rebs sought out the local photographer. "My uniform being made," recently promoted Confederate Lieutenant McHenry Howard recalled, "in the pride of my heart I had my picture taken to be sent home." Ohioan Oscar Ladley's mother admonished her son, "When you go to Washington if you get your Photograph taken I wish you would get a dozen or more if they dont cost too much. The Girls can hardly wait till they get here."

Photographs of commanding officers and military celebrities were in great demand as *cartes-de-visite*. One-armed Union General Philip Kearny was surprised that his wife liked one of the calling-card images he sent home. "I thought it made me look old and pallid, thin and nasty," he wrote. "A little namby pamby, with theatrically fierce eyes." But sometimes a photographer's skill could seemingly improve a subject's physical reality. When he saw his commanding general in the flesh,

Massachusetts Private Robert Carter remarked that George McClellan "is not half so handsome as his photographs at the North would seem to indicate."

Dozens of itinerant photographers flocked to the armies in search of business during lulls in military activity, particularly during the long winter months when the opposing forces hunkered down in canvas and log huts. Writing home in January of 1862, Union Colonel Robert McAllister noted that one cameraman was "making two or three hundred dollars a day" in the camp of the New Jersey Brigade alone. Sometimes entire regiments would pose for the camera, leaving a pictorial record of the scale and panoply of mid-nineteenth century tactics that had yet to come to grips with warfare's deadly new technology.

America's Civil War was the first conflict in which photographers consciously sought to capture war in all its horrors. By the spring of 1862, Mathew Brady's talented crew of photographic "operatives"— Alexander Gardner, Timothy O'Sullivan, George N. Barnard, and James F. Gibson, among others—were actively following the armies, hauling their chemicals, fragile glass plates, and bulky wooden cameras in portable darkrooms. They recorded the gruesome aftermath of battle, and displayed in the picture galleries of Manhattan and Washington a shocking vision of crowded hospitals and the corpse-strewn fields of Antietam, Gettysburg, and Petersburg.

"Let him who wishes to know what war is look at this series of illustrations," Oliver Wendell Holmes wrote of Gardner's Antietam views. "The sight of these pictures is a commentary on civilization such as the savage might well triumph to show its missionaries." "We recognized the battlefield as a reality, but a remote one, like a funeral next door," one New York reporter observed. "Mr. Brady has brought home the terrible earnestness of war. If he has not brought bodies and laid them in our dooryards, he has done something very like it."

Eight months after Lewis Bissell and his comrades posed for the "daguerrian artist" at Alexandria, a third of the regiment lay dead or wounded on the ravaged field of Cold Harbor. Bissell wrote home to let his family know he was still alive. He told of the bloody charge, of the death of his colonel, and the loss of friends who were "like brothers to each other and to us." And then he echoed the feelings of every soldier, Union and Confederate, when he wrote, "If there is ever again any rejoicing in this world, it will be when this war is over. One who has never been under fire has no idea of war."

More than a century and a quarter later, as we gaze at these inscrutable faces with all their pride and innocence, it is hard not to feel an uncanny intimacy with those who were "like brothers to each other and to us."

MUSTER IN

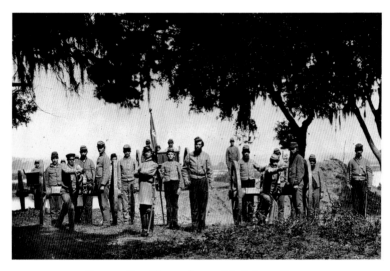

Commanding officer and men of the Palmetto Battery,
Confederate States Army, a unit that served near Charleston, South Carolina,
during most of the war. The photograph probably dates from 1863.

Politicians on one side said it was a war to save the Union. A few of them even took the largely unpopular stand that the war was being fought to save the Union *and* free the slaves. On the other side, politicians said it was a war to defend the rights of individual states against the tyranny of the federal government. They said their "sacred soil" was being invaded.

Politicians on both sides spoke of honor and of glory. These were words, and on both sides, in the decade preceding the war, there were plenty of words: *Union, abolition, states' rights, slavery, duty, sacred, glory, honor.* Both sides also had their fanatics. The North had John Brown, an Ohioan who moved to Kansas in 1855 to help win that state for antislavery forces and then made a name for himself by murdering five pro-slavery men in retaliation for an earlier pro-slavery raid against the abolitionists of Lawrence, Kansas. He planned to invade the South in order to free the slaves, and, toward that end, in 1859, he raided the U.S. Arsenal at Harpers Ferry, Virginia. Robert E. Lee, commanding a company of U.S. Marines, killed ten of Brown's twenty-one men, including two of his sons, and captured Brown, who was tried, convicted of treason, and executed on December 2, 1859.

The South had the likes of old Edmund Ruffin. A vituperative, virulent, voluble secessionist newspaper editor, he joined, at age sixty-seven, a private South Carolina regiment called the Palmetto Guards. When this organization, with others, looked across the harbor to Fort Sumter in the predawn hours of April 12, 1861, it was (as far as anyone could tell) Ruffin who pulled the lanyard that let fly the first shot against the fort from Stevens Battery on Cummings Point. (Ruffin fired his last shot in 1865, when he put a pistol to his head and blew his brains out.)

Few expected much of a war to result from the words of politicians and the acts of fanatics. Surely, one side or the other would back down. Most people thought that war, if it came at all, would be fought and won in a matter of weeks or, perhaps, months. Those few who faced the future with fear were viewed as nervous, moody types, like William Tecumseh Sherman. He had served in the Mexican War, then left the Army back in 1853 to become first a banker in California, then a lawyer. Fed up with civilian life, he applied for readmission to the Army but instead was recommended as superintendent of a military school in Louisiana.

That is where he was when word of South Carolina's secession reached him. It was Christmas Eve of 1860, and he was dining with the academy's classics professor, a Virginian. Sherman glared across the table at his dinner companion. "This country will be drenched in blood," the superintendent seethed, "and God only knows how it will end. It is all folly, madness, a crime against civilization! You people speak so lightly of war; you don't know what you're talking about. War is a terrible thing!"

You couldn't prove that from this war's first battle, which, full of thunder as it was, boded a gentlemanly contest. Confederate General P. G. T. Beauregard sent two men rowing under a flag of truce out to Fort Sumter in Charleston Harbor. They presented commandant Major Robert Anderson with a most chivalrous note demanding surrender of the fort. "All proper facilities will be afforded for the removal of yourself and command," the note announced, "together with company arms and property, and all private property, to any post in the United States which you may select. The flag which you have upheld so long and with so much fortitude, under the most trying circumstances, may be saluted by you on taking it down." (Nor were the opposing commanders strangers. Anderson had been Beauregard's artillery instructor at West Point.)

To Beauregard's note Anderson responded with commensurate chivalry: the general, Anderson replied, had made "a demand with which I regret that my sense of honor, and of my obligations to my government, prevent my compliance." Handing the two rowboat-borne messengers this reply, he

declared to them: "Gentlemen, if you do not batter us to pieces, we shall be starved out in a few days."

Four more rowers called on Anderson after midnight on April 12 with a warning that bombardment was about to commence. Barring further orders or supply from "my government," Anderson replied, he would, indeed, evacuate the fort by the fifteenth.

No, Beauregard's men declared, commence evacuation now, for the bombardment would begin in one hour.

Following Edmund Ruffin's shot, through Friday and into Saturday, some 4,000 rounds were lobbed against Fort Sumter. After this two-day cannonade, content that honor and duty had been served, Anderson surrendered. Incredibly, no one had been hurt.

Or, rather, the casualties came after the battle. Roger Pryor, like Edmund Ruffin, was a "fire-eater"—as ardent secessionists were called—a Virginian who had exhorted South Carolinians to "strike a blow." Now he was given the honor of acting as one of Beauregard's emissaries sent to preside over the surrender of the fort. Seated at a table in Sumter's empty hospital, waiting while a clerk put the surrender terms in writing, he became thirsty. A bottle was close at hand, the fire-eater seized it, and polished off the contents. It must have tasted strange, for he paused now to read the label: iodine of potassium. Realizing that he had been poisoned, Pryor sought the fort's surgeon, who hauled him outside, pumped his stomach, and saved his life. That was the Confederacy's first casualty.

The Union suffered its first losses the next day. Abiding by the surrender terms as originally offered, the Rebels allowed Anderson to salute the flag he had served. Accordingly, the commandant ordered a fifty-gun volley. A stray ember touched off some powder, which exploded, injuring five and killing one. Union Private Daniel Hough was the first to fall in the Civil War. By the end of this war that had commenced so impetuously, then ceremoniously, then almost comically, more than one-third of the men and boys who fought for the North or the South would prove William Tecumseh Sherman right. They would lie wounded or dead.

Behind the innocence, the ignorance, the impetuosity, and the ideals are the faces of men and women caught in a destiny at once intensely personal and inhumanly indifferent to personality and persons. With the faces go the words—not the public language of *honor, duty, glory,* and the rest, but words addressed to family or, in an immediate and intimate way, to posterity: the language of letters, diaries, and autobiography.

Posterity. No American war, perhaps no war fought anywhere or at any time, has spoken to "posterity" more clearly, immediately, and compellingly than the American Civil War. It was a horrible truth soon reduced to cliche: a *civil* war was war between brother and brother. Just as these brothers were divided by mere geography—not the hemispherical geography of twentieth-century warfare, but the intimate geography of this river versus that stream, that valley against this hill, the geography of a day's march—so we are separated from them by mere time, a little more than a hundred years in the history of a nation little more than two hundred years old.

At the beginning of the war, the Union Army consisted of 16,000 officers and men—less 313 officers whose consciences compelled them to go with the South. The Confederate Army started with zero, of course. A "regular" army—the Army of the Confederate States of America—was established by act of the Confederate Provisional Congress on March 6, 1861. But this "regular" army never came into existence as such. The "Rebel" troops the Federal Army fought were soldiers of the volunteer or Provisional Army that had been established by acts of February 28 and March 6. Until April 1862, when the Confederate government passed a conscription act, soldiers entered the Provisional Army not directly, but through the individual states.

By the end of the war, 2,128,948 men had served in the Union Army (359,528 are known to have died). Of these, only 75,215 were regulars—that is, soldiers by vocation. Just under two million were volunteers, 46,347 were draftees, and 73,607 were substitutes (for the conscription laws of both sides permitted a draftee to hire a surrogate soldier to serve in his place). The average strength of the Union Army, according to one prominent authority, was a little over 1.5 million.

The Confederate forces kept poor records, and much of what little was recorded burned in the fires that ravaged a conquered Richmond. Estimates of the strength of the Confederate Army range from 600,000 to 1,500,000; the most generally accepted figure is a little over a million, about 200,000 of whom died.

From these figures, it is not difficult to understand why the generations following the Civil War have all felt such kinship with the warriors. The combatants were not professional soldiers. They were not hirelings of a warlike state. They were citizens, born and raised with no intention of taking up arms. The professions and trades they left were ours: doctor, lawyer, farmer, clerk, broker—over one hundred different occupations are listed on Southern muster rolls, three hundred on Northern. The relationships they suspended are familiar to us: husband to wife, lover to lover, brother to brother. Their lives were our lives—interrupted by a long and deadly storm.

In the great world wars of the twentieth century, men were often uprooted from familiar surroundings and thrust into an army of strangers. This was not the case in the Civil War. Companies of infantry (units of sixty-five to a hundred men) were usually raised in a single locale, which often meant that troops serving together knew one another well. Fathers, sons, brothers, and best friends frequently soldiered in the same company. This may well have boosted morale, but it also meant that one sooner or later bore witness to the death or injury of a relative or friend.

Although, in the North, African Americans agitated for the right to fight from the very beginning of the war, it was not until the autumn of 1862 that black troops were permitted to join the Union Army (in wholly segregated units commanded by white officers). In the South, during the final, desperate months of the war, the Confederate Congress authorized the recruitment of 300,000 black soldiers. However, the Southern citizenry did not welcome them (a newly mustered unit marching through the streets of Richmond was greeted with mud slung by outraged whites), and no African American Confederate soldiers were ever committed to battle.

The typical soldier on either side was a white Protestant, a farmer, unmarried, aged eighteen to twenty-nine. There were, however, also much older men: Edmund Ruffin, aged sixty-seven, and Curtis King, who enlisted in the 37th Iowa at the age of eighty. And there were much younger: Charles C. Hay joined an Alabama regiment at age eleven, and Edward Black joined the 21st Indiana as a nine-year-old musician. While the majority of men on both sides were native born, one out of four Northern soldiers was a first- or second-generation immigrant, mostly of German or Irish origin. Three brigades of Cherokees, Choctaws, Chickasaws, and Seminoles fought for the Confederacy, while one brigade of Creeks enlisted in the Union cause. (The Confederate Army included among its brigadiers the Cherokee leader Stand Watie, whose command was the last Confederate unit to surrender, laying down arms fully a month after hostilities had generally ceased.)

The spirit of these citizen soldiers was, by and large, extraordinary. On both sides, acts of heroism were more common than instances of cowardice, and volunteers outnumbered

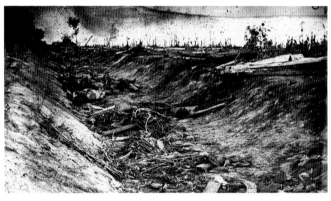

Dead Confederates in the Sunken Road, called Bloody Lane, Antietam

conscripts by a wide margin. However, as the war ground on, the rate of desertion increased, and the gap between voluntary enlistment and conscription progressively narrowed. By the end of the war, one of every ten Federal troops had deserted, as had one in seven Confederates. As voluntary enlistments lagged, both sides offered bounties as enticements to join up. This practice spawned a new class of criminals who enlisted, claimed their bounty, deserted, enlisted elsewhere, collected another bounty, and repeated the cycle as often as they dared. In the later years of the war, deserters were punished severely, often at the receiving end of a firing squad. However, relatively few were ever caught.

In April 1862, the Confederacy enacted a draft law, and the Union followed with a conscription act the next year. On both sides, most men conceded the necessity of conscription. Far less tolerable, however, was the manner in which the laws were administered. In the South, exemption from the draft was granted to owners or overseers of twenty or more slaves, effectively exempting from service the well-to-do. The less affluent Southerner, who had supported the war as a fight against Northern tyranny, now saw himself fighting to maintain the hegemony of the landed gentry.

Both North and South also allowed individuals to make a cash payment in lieu of military service, or to hire a substitute. The "commutation fee" for Union conscripts was $300, a substantial sum in an era when a common laborer earned about a dollar a day, and privately hiring a substitute was not much cheaper. In the North, this inequity led to a wave of defeatism and draft riots. New York City, which had never wholeheartedly rallied 'round the flag, erupted into near revolution on July 13, 1863, and an orgy of burning, looting, and killing consumed the next several days. Masses of Irish immigrants, outraged by the draft law and by the antici- pated influx of emancipated slaves who would "steal" their jobs, turned the draft riot into a race riot. It took a detach- ment of General Meade's Gettysburg veterans to put down the insurrection.

Not that commanding officers were delighted to receive the conscripts. It was reported that, of 186 conscripts assigned to a Massachusetts regiment, 115 deserted, six were discharged as disabled, twenty-six were transferred to naval ser- vice, and one was killed in action. "Depraved" and "degenerate" are words one often reads in connection with con- scripts, paid substitutes, and bounty enlistees. Commissioned as well as non-commissioned officers despaired of waging a war with such men, let alone winning one.

Even the best soldiers, the volunteers, balked at disci- pline. In many cases, with companies that had been raised locally, those now charged with command had been friends, neighbors, or even subordinates in civilian life. Learning to take orders from such as these was a difficult adjustment. Even where this was not a problem, officers tended to be as inexperienced as the men they were supposed to lead, which sometimes resulted in mere incompetence, but often manifested itself as pomposity or even brutality, neither of which has ever sat well with American soldiers. Finally, nineteenth-century America, North and South, was nonmilitary by nature, and its citizens were imbued with markedly independent inclinations.

This independence of spirit is not to be confused with romantic notions of rugged frontiersmen willing and able to fight but steadfastly refusing to be led. Few soldiers on either side could be called frontiersmen. They were farmers, laborers, clerks, and the like. Most had left comfortable homes, few had much affection for the outdoor life, and fewer still had experience with firearms. One evidence of the latter is the fact that the astound- ingly bad rations doled out to the armies of both sides rarely prompted the logical alternative of hunting one's supper.

Just how bad were Civil War rations? Even when rela- tively plentiful, they ran the short gamut from absolutely unappealing to inedible to deadly. One Union staple, hardtack, which soldiers called "sheet-iron crackers" or "teeth dullers," was a half-inch-thick, three-inch-square cracker fabled for its stale- ness. One rumor circulated to the effect that the rations had been warehoused since the Mexican War. Another story was that the initials "B.C.," which were stamped on crates of the stuff, stood not for "brigade commissary," but referred to the date of manufacture. If the soldiers found hardtack well-nigh inedible, however, maggots relished it, so thoroughly infesting supplies that the crackers were sometimes christened "worm castles."

Meat rations were, if anything, even worse. "Fresh" meat was often flyblown before it reached the men. Preserved meat—pickled beef and "salt junk" pork—was, at best, foul smelling and awful tasting, and, at worst, deadly. Varying degrees of food poisoning were commonplace among Civil War soldiers, though it is impossible to determine whether the dysentery endemic to camps was due more to bad food, bad sanitation, or some combination of the two. Fresh fruit and veg- etables were so rare in the enlisted man's diet that scurvy posed a serious threat to both sides. When the Union soldier could stand no more of hardtack and rancid meat, and the Confederate soldier finally tired of cornbread (in good times) or starvation (in bad), there was the option of foraging—a polite term for filching poultry, hogs, sweet potatoes, flour, meal, and the like from local farms, homes, and stores.

Hunting, as has been mentioned, was rarely seen as a viable means of obtaining food. For one thing, game in the vicinity of a camp or battle tended to be scarce. There was also the chance of getting captured or killed by the enemy. More to the point, however, is the fact that few Civil War soldiers ever got good enough at handling a gun to bag a meal. True, they were trained to shoot in the Army, but with arms and ammunition in short supply (especially in the South), they were often trained using sticks instead of muskets. If muskets were available, they were most likely of the aged and obsolescent smoothbore kind, and ammunition for target practice was issued in a most miserly way.

General U. S. Grant witnessed one target practice of the 14th Illinois at which 157 of 160 shots fired were misses. That was typical. It has been calculated that the average Civil War soldier consumed 900 pounds of lead and 240 pounds of powder for each of the enemy he killed. Often, it seems, in the heat of battle, soldiers went through the cumbersome process of loading their weapons only to fail at last to fire them. Some 27,500 muskets were collected on the field after Gettysburg. Of these, more than 12,000 contained two charges. Another 6,000 contained three to ten charges and balls. One was found stuffed with no fewer than twenty-three rounds.

These are facts. The lot of the Civil War soldier was disorder, discomfort, disease, and death. The facts, however, fall short of the whole truth. There was waste, ineptitude, disloyalty, and desertion on both sides. But, as James I. Robertson, Jr. has observed in

his *Soldiers Blue and Gray* (the source of many of the statistics given above), for every instance of failure of fortitude, one finds a hundred or more examples of heroism. The Civil War soldier faced combat on a scale unprecedented. The burgeoning technology developed at the mid-nineteenth-century apogee of the Industrial Revolution turned out firearms in staggering numbers, fashioned bigger and more destructive artillery, and hammered and forged the naval killing machine known as the ironclad. It also equipped (however inadequately), fed (however poorly), and transported (however uncomfortably) vast numbers of fighting men.

Despite the unprecedented mass of military hardware and the unyielding onslaught of human numbers, this immense war was finally and intensely intimate, always driven, it seems, to reduce combat to its essentials. Men shot at one another from close range, a few hundred yards at most. Often, they were near enough to "club" their muskets, holding them by the barrel so that the stock could be used as a weapon that would have been familiar to a prehistoric man. At times, the fighting was even more primitive, a matter of bare hand to bare hand.

It has been said that the troops of the Union and the Confederacy were among the worst soldiers America ever fielded, but perhaps the best fighters. For four years they fought through terror, pain, and discouragement. They fought from motives founded in a sense of place, a notion of inalienable rights, a reverence for honor, and a fear of incurring dishonor. Having been born to the blessings of liberty and varying degrees of plenty, they were hardly ripe for soldiering. But when the time came, North and South, they fought without compromise, fought their foemen and their brothers, hand-to-hand, eye-to-eye, face-to-face.

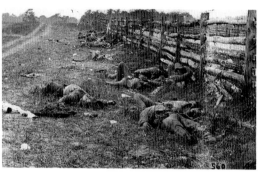

Dead Confederates along the Hagerstown Pike, Antietam

MY BROTHER'S FACE

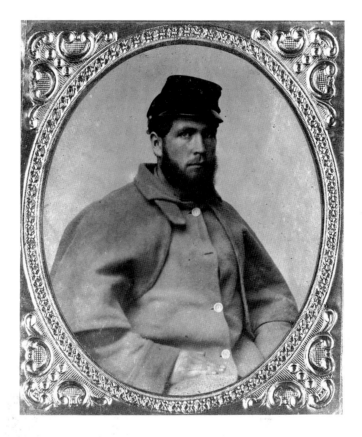

THE FALL OF FORT SUMTER

April 12–13, 1861

The first shot of the Civil War was fired against Fort Sumter, in Charleston Harbor, at 4:30 a.m. While the gentry of Charleston watched from that city's fashionable Battery, Confederate artillery bombarded the fort until, his ammunition exhausted, Sumter commandant Major Robert Anderson surrendered. He and his garrison were permitted to withdraw with full military honors, and the Stars and Bars were raised over the fort's battered interior.

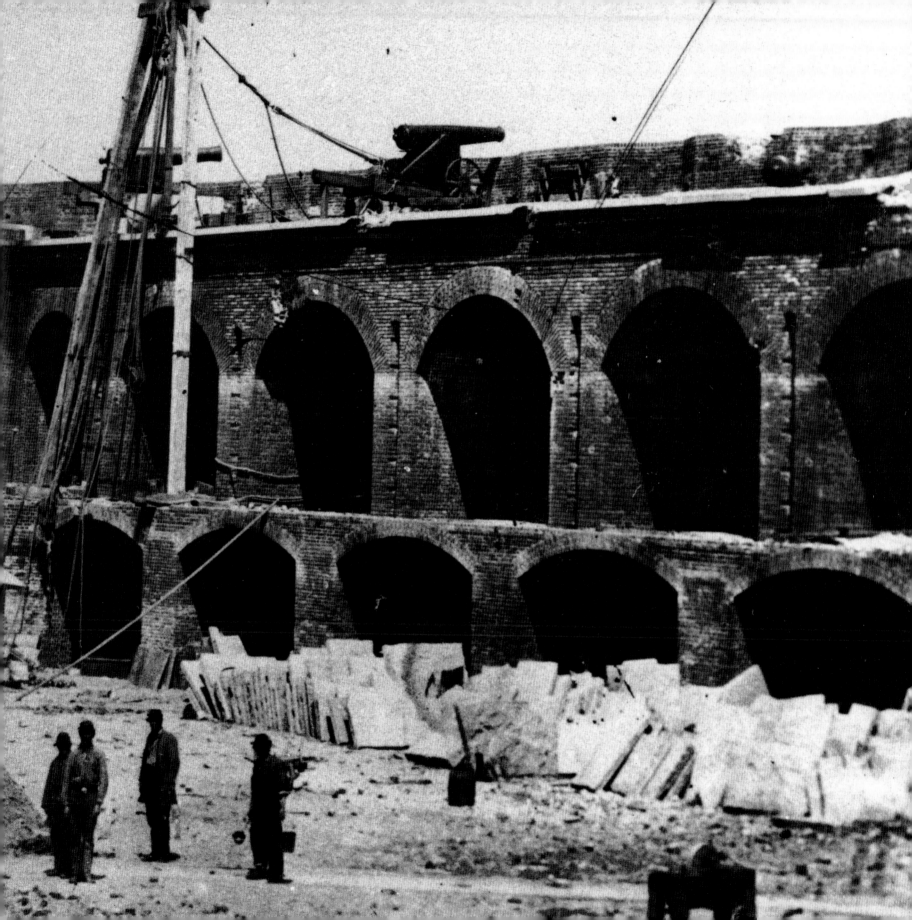

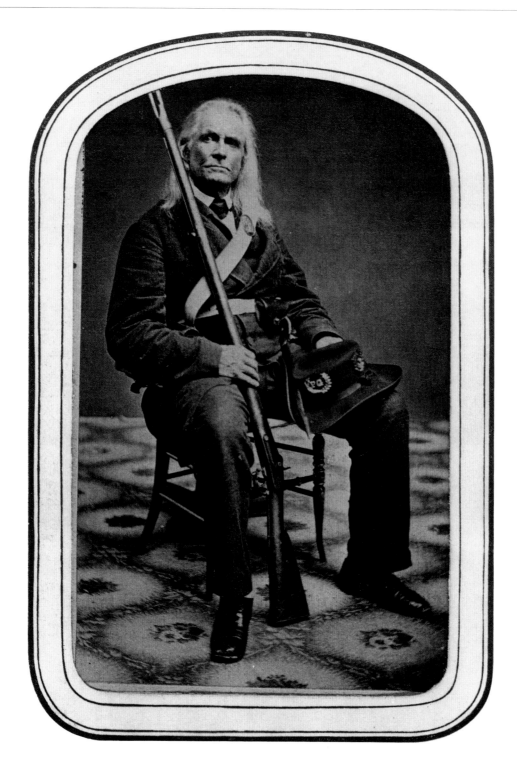

Edmund Ruffin (1794-1865), whom one historian describes as an "ancient and ardent secessionist," claimed credit for having fired the first shot of the Civil War. Actually, Captain George S. James fired a signal gun first, but it is probable that Ruffin pulled the lanyard that let fly the first shot from Stevens Battery on Cummings Point. He commemorated the event in this photograph, posing with a U.S. Model 1842 musket and the hat and accoutrements of the Palmetto Guards, the Charleston militia outfit in which the sixty-seven-year-old man served during the bombardment. If Ruffin was an old and defiant man at the start of the war, he was an old and broken man by war's end. But still fanatically defiant. In 1865, with his home, cause, and country in ruins (a Federal soldier had scrawled along a wall: "This house belonged to a Ruffinly son-of-a-bitch"), Ruffin refused to accept life under Union authority. He blew his brains out, having first written a suicide note:

And now with my latest writing and utterance . . . I here repeat . . . my unmitigated hatred to Yankee rule . . . and the perfidious, malignant and vile Yankee race.

The mission of taking Fort Sumter fell to Brigadier General Pierre Gustave Toutant Beauregard, commanding the Confederate defenses at Charleston Harbor. This photograph dates from a later period than Fort Sumter, most likely 1862-64, about the time that Arthur James Lyon Fremantle, lieutenant colonel of Her Majesty's Coldstream Guards, visited Beauregard, an event he recorded in his diary:

At 1 p.m. I called on General Beauregard, who is a man of middle height, about forty-seven years of age. He would be very youthful in appearance were it not for the color of his hair, which is much grayer than his earlier photographs represent. Some persons account for the sudden manner in which his hair turned gray by allusions to his cares and anxieties during the last two years. The real and less romantic reason is to be found in the rigidity of the Yankee [naval] blockade, which interrupts the arrival of articles of toilet. He has a long straight nose, handsome brown eyes, and a dark mustache without whiskers, and his manners are extremely polite. He is a New Orleans Creole, and French is his native language.

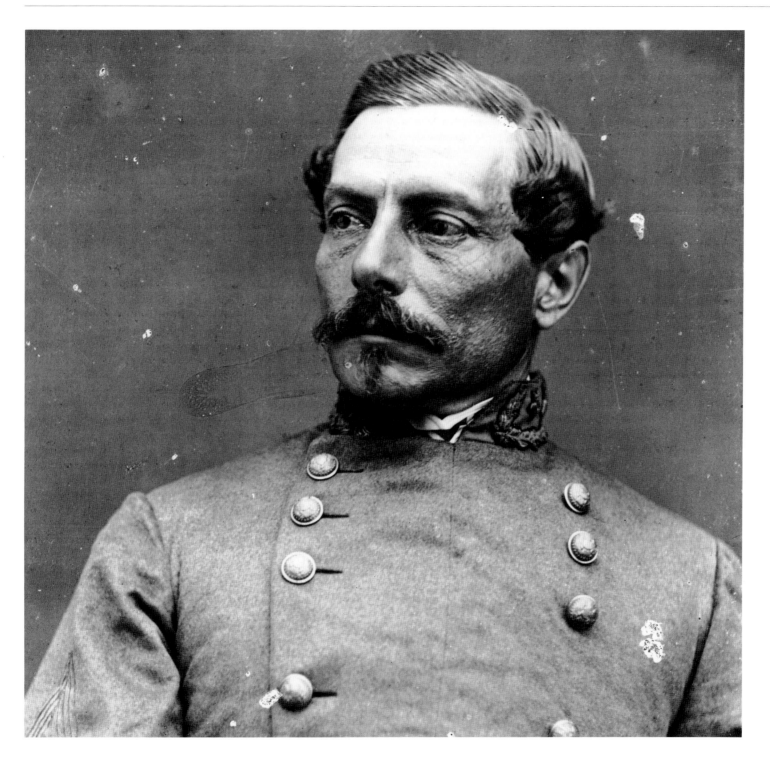

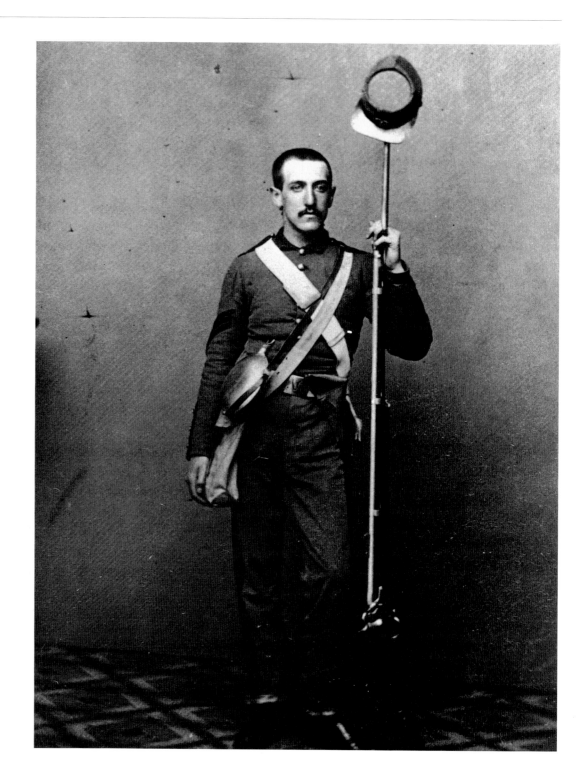

Many young men rushed to arms at the outbreak of war. Sergeant Oscar Ryder, pictured here in 1861, joined the 7th New York State Militia, a famous prewar unit that functioned as a club for the social elite as much as a unit for potential combat. Members purchased their own uniforms (which were gray) and equipment, except for arms. Ryder's weapon is a U.S. Model 1855 Rifle Musket, far newer, more efficient, and accurate than the musket Edmund Ruffin posed with. The 7th New York State Militia was mustered into Federal service on April 26, 1861, served in Washington until June 3, when the unit returned to New York City and was mustered out.

In *My Story of the War*, Bostonian Mary A. Livermore recalled a scene that was enacted all across the Union as the North rallied to arms in the wake of Fort Sumter:

As they marched from the railroad stations, they were escorted by crowds cheering vociferously. Merchants and clerks rushed out from stores, bareheaded, saluting them as they passed. Windows were flung up; and women leaned out into the rain, waving flags and handkerchiefs. Horse-cars and omnibuses halted for the passage of the soldiers, and cheer upon cheer leaped forth from thronged doors and windows.

A fez—headgear popular with elite "Zouave" units and incongruously worn here—a hickory shirt, side knife, and revolver have transformed this farm boy into a private of Company F, 4th Michigan Infantry. When he heard the news of Fort Sumter's fall, Theodore Upson—another farm boy, from Indiana—wrote:

Father and I were husking out some corn. We could not finish before it wintered up. When William Cory came across the field (he had been down after the Mail) he was excited and said, "Jonathan the Rebs have fired upon and taken Fort Sumter." Father got white and couldn't say a word.

William said, "The President will soon fix them. He has called for 75,000 men and is going to blockade their ports, and just as soon as those fellows find out that the North means business they will get down off their high horse."

Father said little. We did not finish the corn and drove to the barn. Father left me to unload and put out the team and went to the house. After I had finished I went in to dinner. Mother said, "What is the matter with Father?" He had gone right upstairs. I told her what we had heard. She went to him. After a while they came down. Father looked ten years older. We sat down to the table. Grandma wanted to know what was the trouble. Father told her and she began to cry. "Oh my poor children in the South! How they will suffer! God knows how they will suffer! I knew it would come! Jonathan I told you it would come!"

"They can come here and stay," said Father.

"No they will not do that. There is their home. There they will stay. Oh to think that I should have lived to see the day when Brother should rise against Brother!"

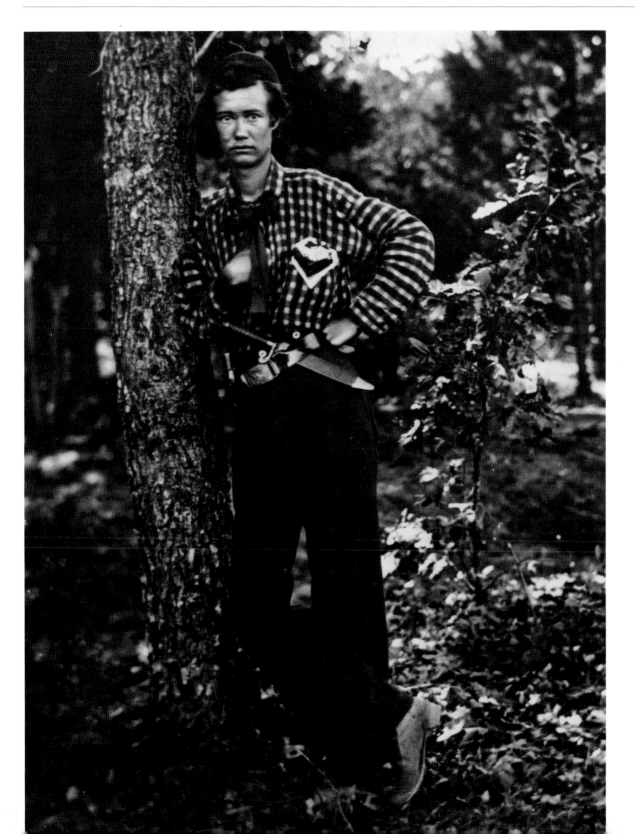

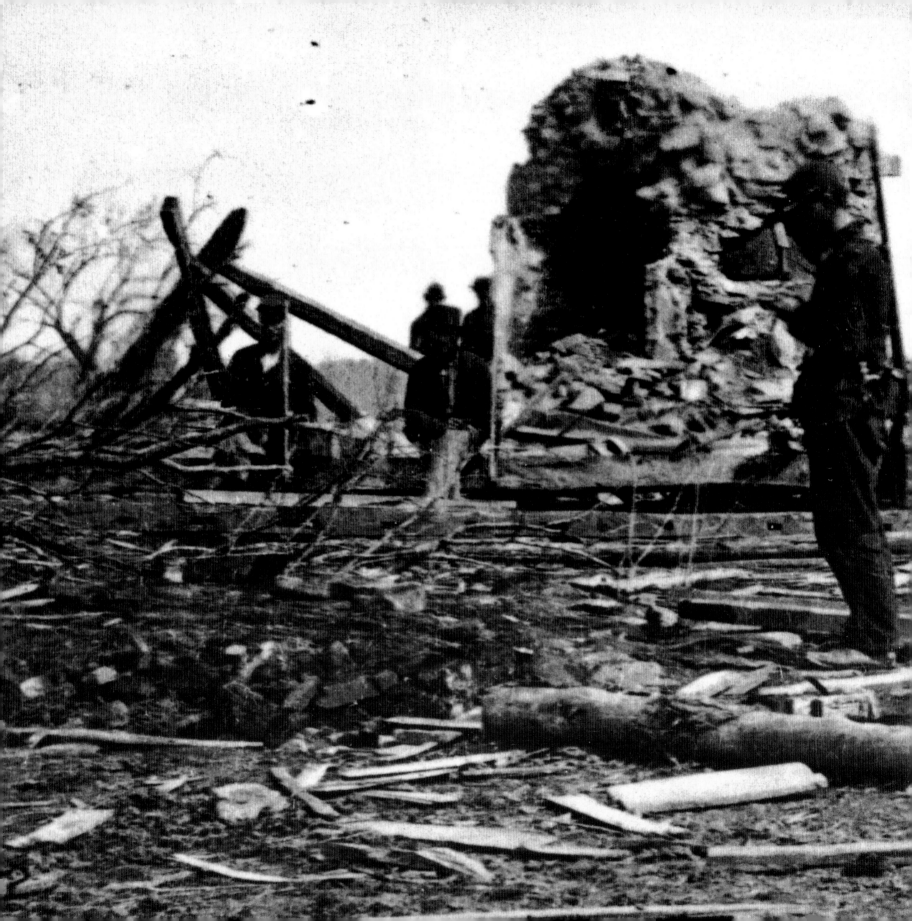

FIRST MANASSAS

July 21, 1861

An almost carnival atmosphere pervaded the opening of the first major battle of the Civil War. On July 21, Washington's high society rode out to nearby Centreville, Virginia, in carriages filled with picnic baskets and bottles of champagne, to view, through field glasses and telescopes, the action three miles off. The Union troops, too, most of them volunteers, had seemed in good spirits on the two-day approach march to battle position through the sweltering summer heat. Every few miles, they broke rank to pick blackberries or gather water.

Confederate General P. G. T. Beauregard had been alerted to the Union advance by means of uncensored newspaper articles and spies, including prominent Washington socialite and Rebel agent Mrs. Rose O'Neal Greenhow. He had thrown up his defenses near a railroad crossing called Manassas Junction. There, across tiny Bull Run Creek, his 20,000 Rebels faced 37,000 Yankees under the command of the prim and proper General Irvin McDowell. The numbers would grow more equitable as Rebel reinforcements, led by General Joseph E. Johnston, arrived from the Shenandoah Valley.

At first the Northerners, cheered on by the civilian onlookers, seemed to carry the day, driving the Rebels from their positions and turning the Confederate left. But the Southerners took heart from the example of one Virginia brigade that held steadfastly to its position on a hill at the center of the Rebel line. The action earned brigade commander General Thomas J. Jackson his nickname, "Stonewall," because his men held their position unwaveringly. The Confederates rallied, and all afternoon the fighting seesawed back and forth. During a massive late-afternoon Confederate counterattack, the Union forces broke and ran—along with their noncombatant cheering section—all the way back to Washington. Jackson had ordered his men to "yell like Furies" as they chased the Yankees, and few of the latter ever forgot the first time they heard the eerie, high-pitched scream that came to be known as the "Rebel Yell."

The battle transformed pretty Manassas into a cratered collection of ruins, such as the remains of the Henry House on Henry House Hill, seen in a photograph taken well after the battle, very early in the spring of 1862.

Rose O'Neal Greenhow, daughter of an aristocratic Maryland family, kin of the Lees, Randolphs, and Calverts, was the Washington widow of Dr. Robert Greenhow, a scholarly Virginia lawyer and State Department official. Through him—and her own irresistible charms—she gained many friends, the overwhelming majority of them male and of considerable consequence in the government of the United States. "I am a Southern woman," she later wrote, "born with revolutionary blood in my veins." A protégé of John C. Calhoun, she became an astoundingly active Confederate spy during the opening months of the war, exploiting her highly placed friends and seducing government and Army officials, ranging from War Department clerks to a United States senator, extracting from them a wealth of military secrets.

In a published memoir, she claimed to have supplied Southern military leaders with nothing less than a steady stream of "verbatim" cabinet reports. Whether this is an exaggeration or not, the information Rose Greenhow communicated on the eve of First Manassas, which included reports of Federal troop movements and strength, was useful enough to merit a note from Confederate spymaster Thomas Jordan on July 23, 1861: "Our President and our General direct me to thank you. The Confederacy owes you a debt."

Soon after First Manassas, Rose was apprehended by private detective turned Federal agent, Allan J. Pinkerton. At first she was placed under house arrest, and, in a "most bravely indeli-cate" letter she sent to friends in South Carolina (which diarist Mary Chesnut read on December 5, 1861), she lavishly detailed the treatment to which she was subjected:

She wants us to know how her delicacy was shocked and outraged [Chesnut wrote in her diary]. That could be done only by most plain-spoken revelations. For eight days she was kept in full sight of men—her rooms wide open—and sleepless sentinels watching by day and by night. Soldiers tramping—looking in at her leisurely by way of amusement.

Beautiful as she is, at her time of life few women like all the mysteries of their toilette laid bare to the public eye.

She says she was worse used than Marie Antoinette when they snatched a letter from the poor queen's bosom.

Later, she was moved, with her youngest daughter, called Little Rose, to Old Capitol Prison, where Mathew B. Brady or an assistant took this daguerreotype. Even after her incarceration, Rose continued to pass messages through her window—until her jailers boarded it up. Those boards, hastily nailed in place, are clearly visible in the photograph. Rose Greenhow was later "paroled" to the South and traveled to Europe, where she published a best-selling memoir. On her return to the Confederacy, while running a Union blockade, she was drowned at the mouth of the Cape Fear River. 🐾

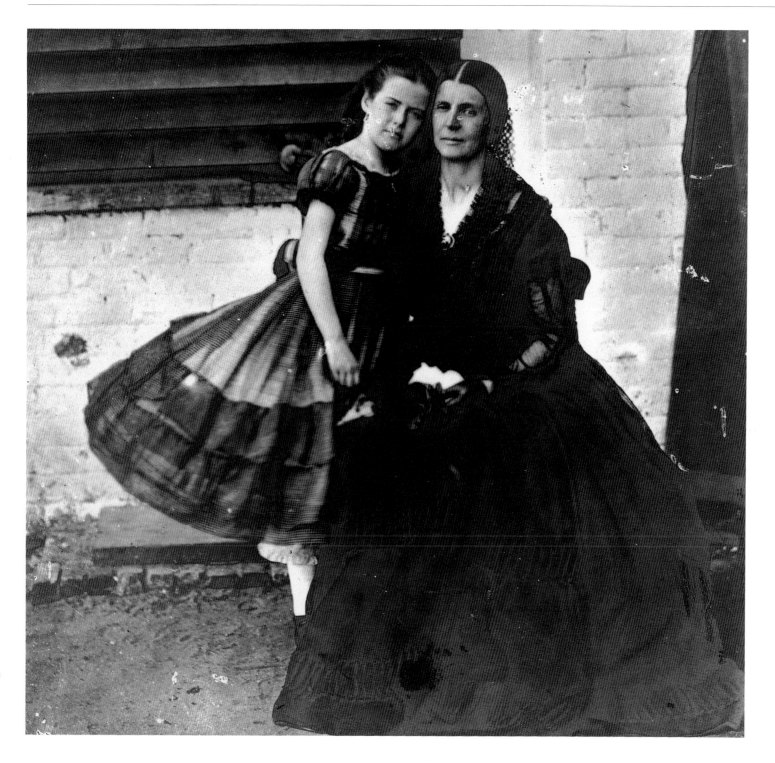

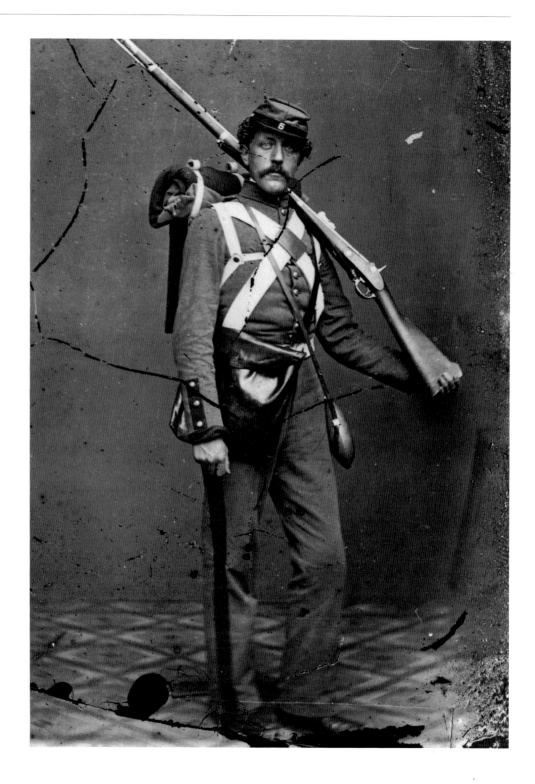

The unidentified volunteer pictured here probably served in a New York militia regiment and is typical of the Union troops who marched to Manassas—well equipped and confident of victory. They were not, however, well trained, nor were they prepared to meet the rigors—let alone horrors—of war, as their commander, Brigadier General Irvin McDowell, observed:

They stopped every moment to pick blackberries or get water; they would not keep in the ranks, order as much as you pleased. When they came where water was fresh, they would pour the old water out of their canteens and fill them with fresh water. They were not used to denying themselves much; they were not used to journeys on foot.

William W. Blackford, an officer attached to Confederate Colonel J. E. B. Stuart's feared Black Horse Cavalry at the first battle of Manassas, describes the approach of New York Zouaves—of which the men pictured here are examples (they most likely served with the 6th or 11th New York). The exotic attire of these soldiers, modeled on the uniforms of French colonial Algerian light infantry troops, was popular with both Northern and Southern regiments; hence Stuart's momentary confusion, noted below:

Colonel Stuart and myself were riding at the head of the column as the grand panorama opened before us, and there right in front, about seventy yards distant, and in strong relief against the smoke beyond, stretched a brilliant line of scarlet—a regiment of New York Zouaves in column of fours, marching out of the Sudley road to attack the flank of our line of battle. Dressed in scarlet caps and trousers, blue jackets with quantities of gilt buttons, and white gaiters, with a fringe of bayonets swaying above them as they moved, their appearance was indeed magnificent. The Sudley road was here in a deep depression and the rear of the column was still hid from view—there were about five hundred men in sight—they were all looking toward the battlefield and did not see us. Waving his saber, Stuart ordered a charge, but instantly pulled up and called a halt and turning to me said, "Blackford, are those our men or the enemy?" I said I could not tell, but I had heard that Beauregard had a regiment of Zouaves from New Orleans, dressed, I had been told, like these men. Just then all doubt was removed by the appearance of their colors, emerging from the road—the Stars and Stripes. I shall never forget the feelings with which I regarded this emblem of our country so long beloved, and now seen for the first time in the hands of a mortal foe. 🏴

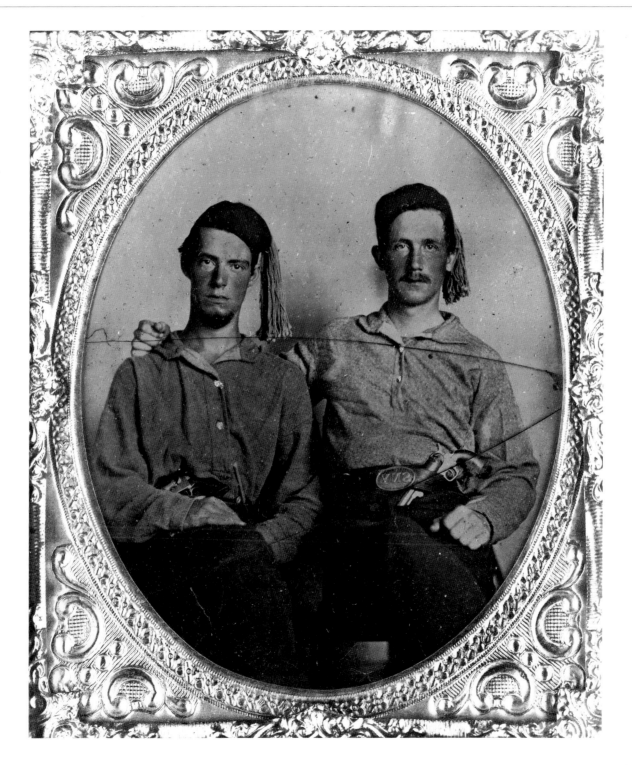

SHILOH

April 6–7, 1862

General Ulysses S. Grant's Army of the Tennessee was encamped on a vulnerable position at Pittsburg Landing, on the Tennessee River, when it was attacked on April 6 by Confederate generals Albert Sidney Johnston and P. G. T. Beauregard. The first twelve hours of battle were consumed in a one-sided struggle between brilliantly led Confederates and disorganized, fragmented Union forces. By the end of Sunday, the Confederates had captured the key position of Shiloh Church and had pushed the Union lines perilously close to the river. Union defeat seemed certain, but Grant, reinforced by General Don Carlos Buell's Army of the Ohio and a division under General Lew Wallace (future author of *Ben-Hur*), counterattacked on Monday morning. Johnston, one of the South's most able and beloved commanders, was killed, and Beauregard, after a ten-hour fight, withdrew his army to Corinth. On balance, Shiloh was a Union victory, but at the staggering cost of 13,000 killed, wounded, captured, or missing out of an army of 55,000. Confederate losses were 11,000 killed, wounded, captured, or missing out of 42,000. In view of such casualties, Abraham Lincoln was pressed to remove Grant. The president resisted, replying, "I can't spare this man; he fights."

The photograph shows Battery B of the 2nd Illinois Light Artillery, which fought at Shiloh from the position pictured here, along the defensive line Grant set up near Pittsburg Landing. Although the unit was described as a light battery, it was equipped with massive 24-pounder siege guns.

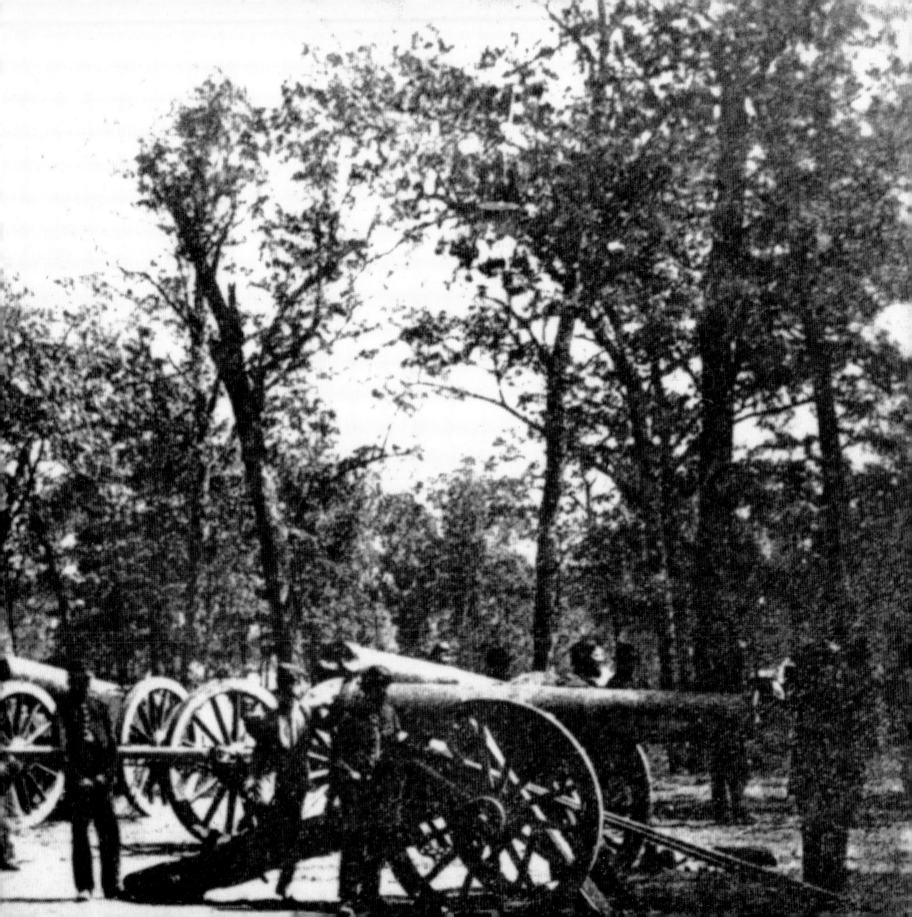

According to Library of Congress files, Private Altman Sampson, of Company C, 29th Georgia Volunteers, fought at Shiloh, dying almost exactly a year after the battle, not of wounds, but of a cause far more common in the Civil War: disease. This information is at variance with Sampson's actual service record, which notes his death from pneumonia on April 27, 1862, barely three weeks after Shiloh, and not in Tennessee, but in Augusta, Georgia. We can only wonder if he fought at Shiloh while ill, or, since he died in Georgia only three weeks after the battle, whether he fought at Shiloh at all. The discrepancy in records is poignant, reminding us that all we know for certain of Altman Sampson was that, like so many others, he fought in the Civil War, he fell ill, he died, and he was young. Of his thoughts and words we know nothing.

A handful of soldiers left something more. John Rowlands was born in Wales, sailed as a cabin boy to Louisiana, and was adopted by Henry Morton Stanley, a New Orleans merchant, whose name Rowlands took for his own when he enlisted in the Dixie Grays. Stanley fought at Shiloh, was captured, and subsequently enlisted in the *Union* artillery. Discharged, he returned to England, but then came back to the United States, where he enlisted in the Union Navy. He is best known for his later exploits as the journalist and explorer who found the long-lost African missionary, physician, and explorer Dr. David Livingstone. Stanley recorded this moment from the opening of Shiloh:

Day broke with every promise of a fine day. Next to me, on my right, was a boy of seventeen, Henry Parker. I remember it because, while we stood-at-ease, he drew my attention to some violets at his feet, and said, "It would be a good idea to put a few into my cap. Perhaps the Yanks won't shoot me if they see me wearing such flowers, for they are a sign of peace."

"Capital," said I, "I will do the same."

We plucked a bunch, and arranged the violets in our caps. The men in the ranks laughed at our proceedings, and had not the enemy been so near, their merry mood might have been communicated to the army.

. . . Before we had gone five hundred paces, our serenity was disturbed by some desultory firing in front. It was then a quarter-past five. "They are at it already," we whispered to each other. . . . Within a few minutes, there was another explosive burst of musketry, the air was pierced by many missiles, which hummed and pinged sharply by our ears, pattered through the tree-tops, and brought twigs and leaves down on us. "Those are bullets," Henry whispered with awe.

. . . I, at last, saw a row of little globes of pearly smoke streaked with crimson, breaking-out with spurtive quickness, from a long line of blue figures in front; and simultaneously, there broke upon our ears an appalling crash of sound, the series of fusillades following one another with startling suddenness, which suggested to my somewhat moidered sense a mountain upheaved, with huge rocks tumbling and thundering down a slope, and the echoes rumbling and receding through space. . . . All the world seemed involved in one tremendous ruin!

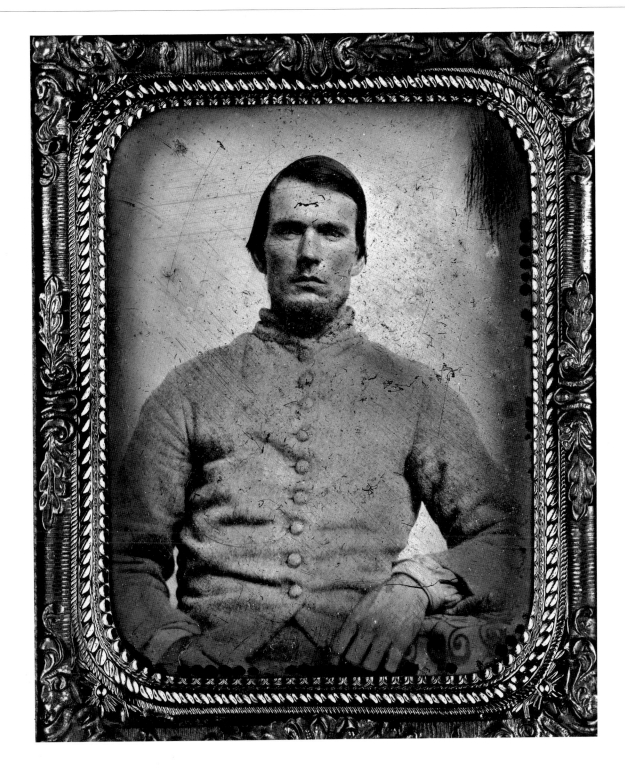

Since many Ohioans fought at Shiloh, perhaps this unidentified member of an Ohio regiment was there. He is posed with an obsolescent weapon, either a U.S. Model 1821 musket converted to percussion or a Model 1842, which may represent his regiment's equipment or may have been merely a photographer's prop. The fight, however, was real enough, as a Federal captain recalled:

After our regiment had been nearly annihilated, and [we] were compelled to retreat under a galling fire, a boy was supporting his dying brother on one arm . . . trying to drag him from the field and the advancing foe. He looked at me imploringly and said, "Captain, help him—won't you? Do, captain; he'll live."

I said, "He's shot through the head, don't you see? and can't live. He's dying now."

"O, no he ain't, captain. Don't leave me."

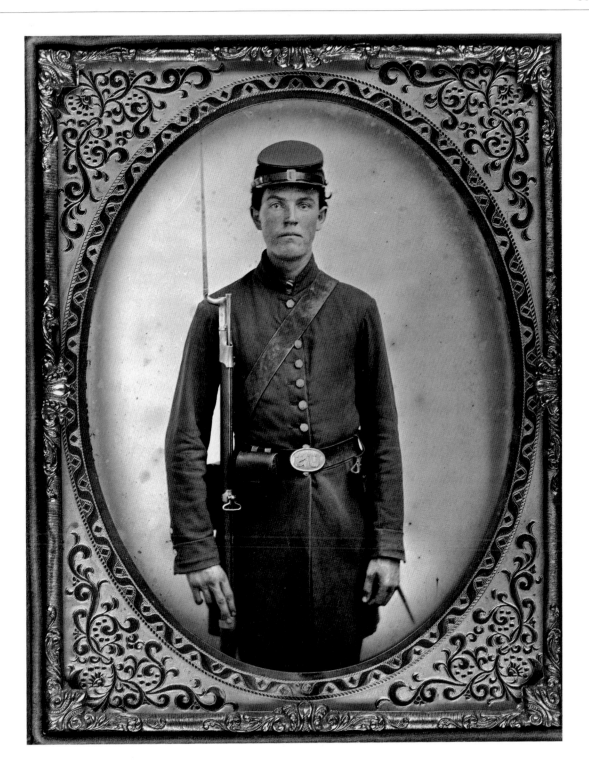

THE PENINSULAR CAMPAIGN

March–July 1862

In the series of battles on the Virginia peninsula known as the Seven Days, which constituted the major action of Union commander George B. McClellan's "Peninsular Campaign," more men were killed or wounded than in all the Civil War battles fought elsewhere during the first half of 1862, including bloody Shiloh. For the first time, Robert E. Lee was placed at the head of a major army, which he renamed the Army of Northern Virginia and which he took on the offensive against the ever-cautious and self-important McClellan. Lee was given the command after Confederate General Joseph E. Johnston was wounded during an early battle at Fair Oaks, a bloody draw on a rainy May 30, just outside Richmond, where fell some 5,000 Union and 6,000 Confederate soldiers. In one of his first moves, Lee sent his cavalry, under the bold command of Brigadier General J. E. B. Stuart, on a spectacular reconnaissance mission around the entire of the Union forces, after which Lee launched a series of daring attacks. The photograph is of a Union artillery position at Casey's Redoubt and "Twin Houses" on the battlefield of the Seven Pines (Fair Oaks). The heaviest fighting on this spot took place on May 31.

On June 26, McClellan had at last mustered the will to mount an attack on Richmond, but Lee hit him first at Mechanicsville in what was to be the first battle of the Seven Days. Lee struck the Union right, and the attack cost him 1,500 men, but he pressed on, determined to drive McClellan off the Virginia peninsula. The fighting lasted a full week at little backwater spots such as Gaines' Mill and Savage's Station and Frayser's Farm. Then, at Malvern Hill on July 1, Union artillery and rifle fire cut the Confederates to ribbons as they came charging up a long slope. During the course of the week, some 15,000 bleeding Rebels were carried to Richmond, where every house was thrown open for the wounded.

By week's end, Lee had lost twice as many men as his adversary, but he had won the psychological advantage. Though all but one of the battles were Union victories, McClellan reacted as if they were defeats, allowing himself and his huge army to be backed down the peninsula until he reached the protection of the Federal gunboats on the James River on July 3. Despite the urging of Union officers, an unnerved McClellan refused to counterattack a foe weakened by the loss of some 20,000 men. As Lee's legend began to spread, crediting him with a knack for surprise, a love of the audacious, and an uncanny, almost clairvoyant, ability to read his enemy's mind, at least one Union officer suggested privately that McClellan was either a coward or a traitor.

Lincoln himself sailed down to see his commanding general three days later, only to hear from McClellan that he had not actually lost, only failed to win because of Lee's superior numbers. When he told his frustrated president that he needed 50,000, perhaps a 100,000 more men, Lincoln at length withdrew McClellan's army from the peninsula and took steps to replace its faint-hearted leader.

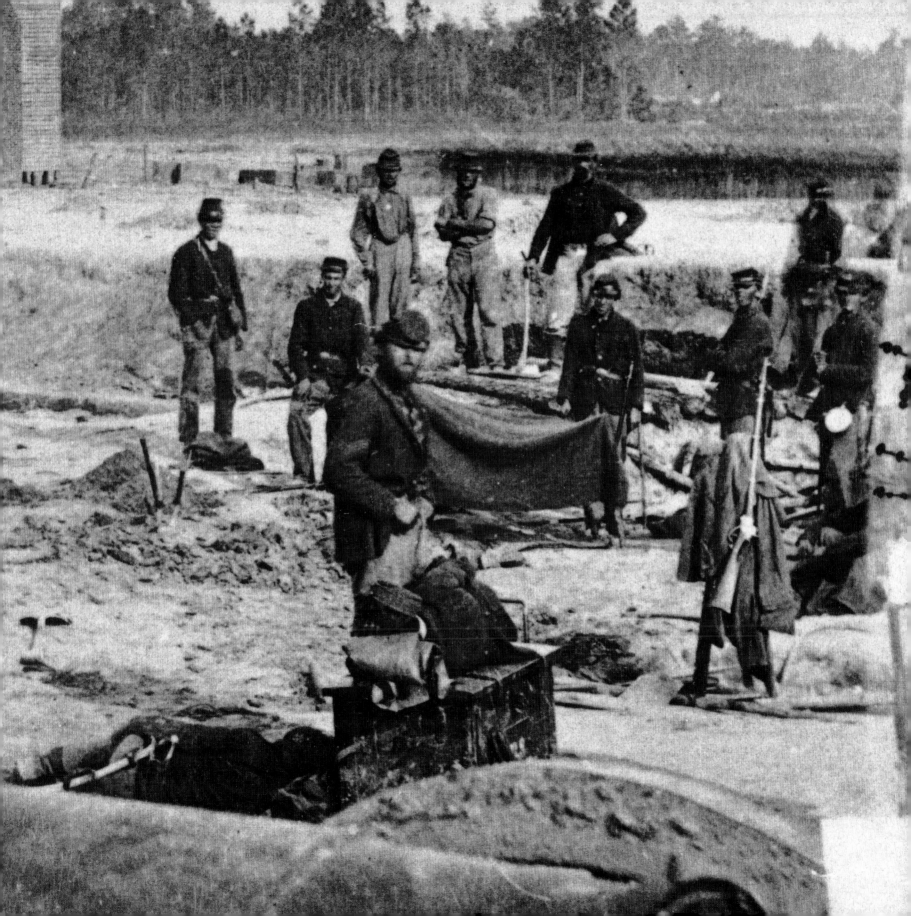

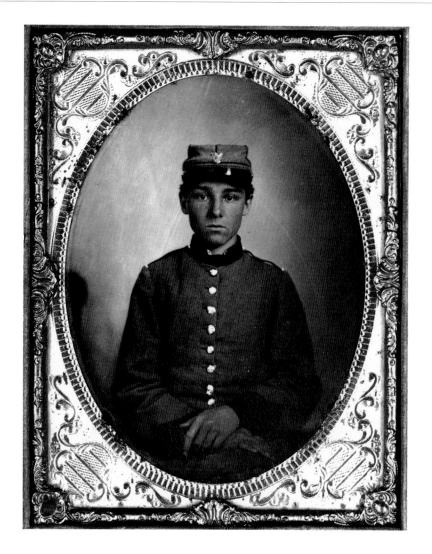

Under a devastating barrage from Federal artillery, Confederate Major General Daniel Harvey Hill was forced to retreat from an assault on Malvern Hill, but he was generous enough to praise the simultaneous—and utterly doomed—advance of the troops commanded by his colleague Major General John B. Magruder:

I never saw anything more grandly heroic than the advance after sunset of the nine brigades under Magruder's orders. Unfortunately, *they did not move together, and were beaten in detail. As each brigade emerged from the woods, from fifty to one hundred guns opened upon it, tearing great gaps in its ranks; but the heroes reeled on—and were shot down by the [infantry supports] at the guns, which a few squads reached. . . . It was not war—it was murder.*

Among the Seven Days' legion of victims was Private Edwin Francis Jamieson, 2nd Louisiana Regiment, whose haunting gaze is one of the most moving images of the Civil War.

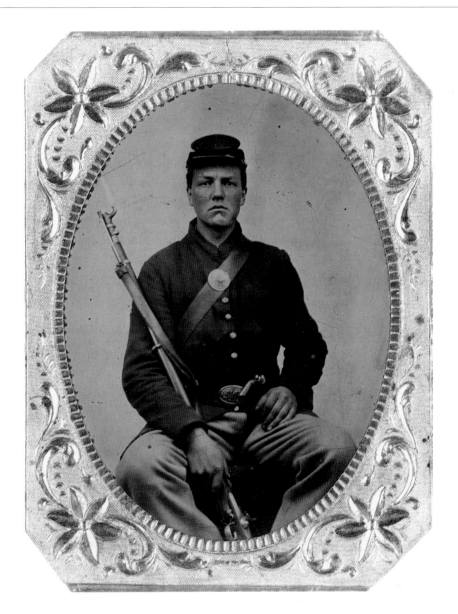

Southern boys like Jamieson fought Northern boys like New York volunteer Private George A. Stryker, pictured here, in the kind of action Warren Lee Goss, a Massachusetts private, described at Malvern Hill:

Night came, yet the fight went on. . . . The lurid flashes of artillery . . . the crackle of musketry, with flashes seen in the distance like fire-flies; the hoarse shriek of the huge shells from the gun-boats . . . made it a scene of terrible grandeur. The ground in front . . . was literally covered with the dead and wounded. At nine o'clock the sounds of the battle died away, and cheer after cheer went up from the victors on the hill.

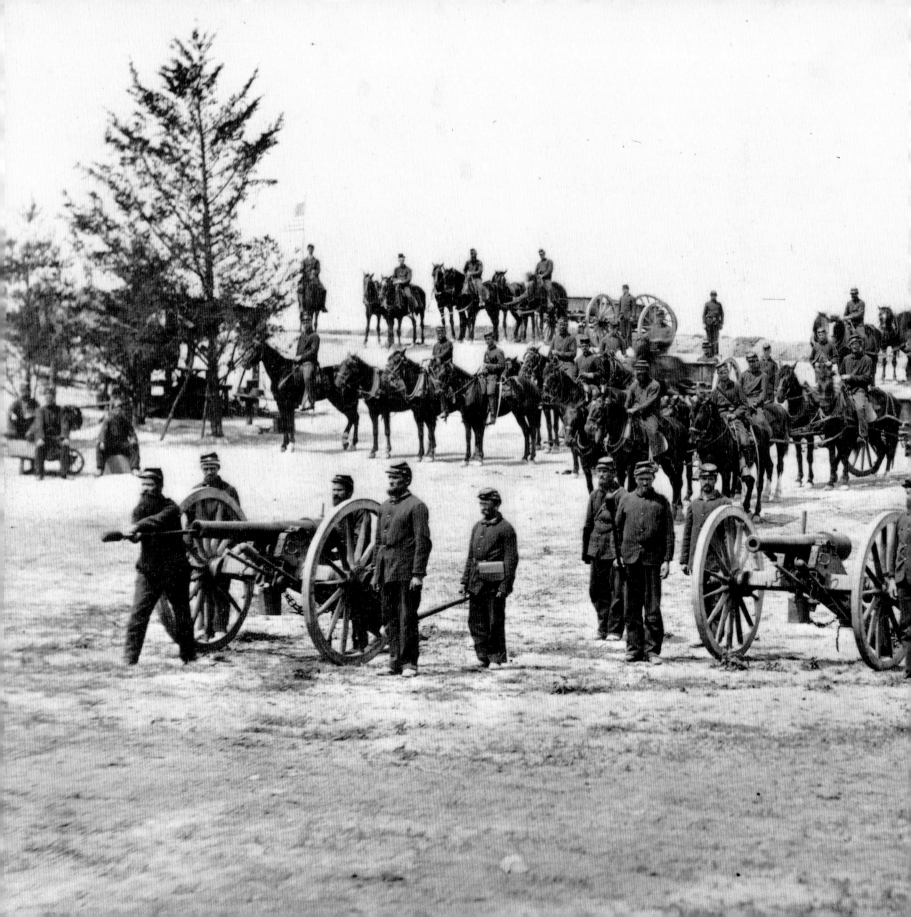

SECOND MANASSAS

August 29–30, 1862

Fed up with McClellan's timidity after the Seven Days campaign, Lincoln finally relieved the Young Napoleon, replacing him with two veterans from the West. Henry "Old Brains" Halleck became General-in-Chief of the United States Army, and John Pope took over McClellan's troops north and west of Richmond. A condescending braggart, Pope was not only unpopular with his fellow officers, he was as despised by the common Union soldier as McClellan was beloved. Confederate soldiers hated Pope for the harshness with which he treated Southern civilians. As soon as it was clear that McClellan no longer threatened Richmond, Lee—again defying traditional military doctrine—split his command in two and headed north to "suppress" the "miscreant" Pope.

Stonewall Jackson caught up with Pope's troops on August 9 at Cedar Mountain near Culpeper Courthouse in Virginia and fought them to a standstill that may be counted a Confederate victory. J. E. B. Stuart struck next, raiding Pope's headquarters, confiscating $35,000 in cash, a notebook indicating the disposition of Union troops, and Pope's dress coat. In a long, clockwise flanking march that was fast becoming a typical Lee stratagem, Jackson first turned west, then east on August 26 to lead his 25,000 men on a remarkable two-day, fifty-six-mile journey to cut Pope's railway communications. Though Herman Haupt, the North's railroading wizard, had the tracks repaired and the trains running within four days, Pope was not equal to Haupt's engineering genius. In fact, while the tracks were being repaired, Pope had lost all trace of Jackson. He found him two days later, ensconced on Stony Ridge, overlooking the Manassas battlefield of the year before.

Boasting he would "bag the whole crowd," Pope launched an attack on August 29. The Rebels held, though late in the battle many of them were reduced to hurling rocks at the Yankees, having run out of bullets. Convinced they would flee, Pope was promising a relentless pursuit for the next day just as the second half of Lee's command, under Longstreet, arrived at 2 P.M. Five divisions stormed into the Union flank along a two-mile front. By the time it had ended, the Union had suffered some 16,000 casualties, more than five times the number killed, wounded, or missing at the first Manassas. Lincoln, his troops demoralized, his cabinet openly critical, his political enemies in an uproar, reluctantly sent the disgraced Pope off to fight Sioux in Minnesota and gave McClellan back his command.

Pennsylvania's "Keystone" artillery, pictured here at drill, was among the Union forces deployed at Second Manassas.

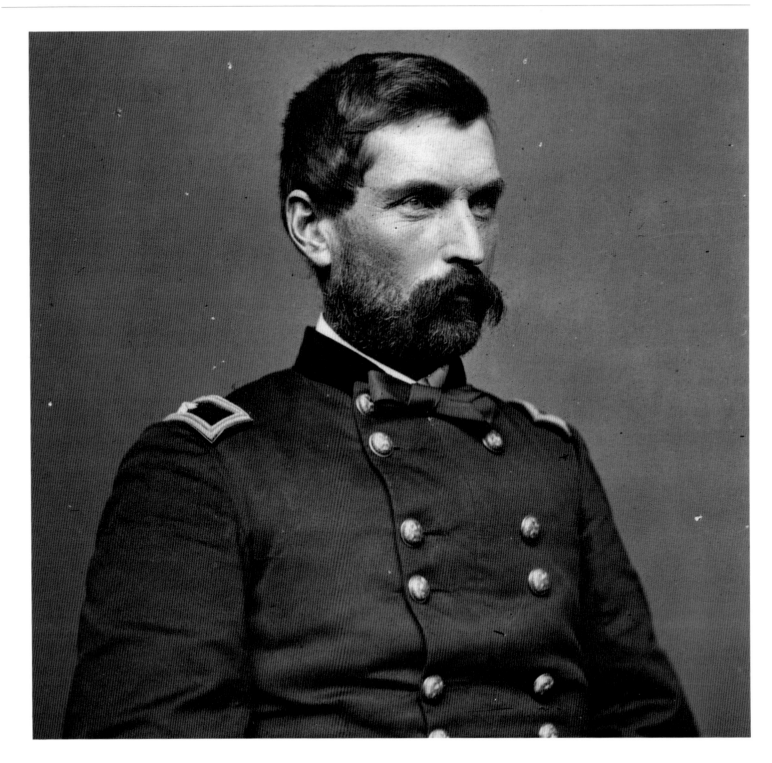

From the relatively distant perspective of Union General John Pope's headquarters, the spectacle of Second Manassas struck D. H. Strother as rather beautiful:

The sparkling lines of musketry shone in the darkness like fireflies in a meadow, while the more brilliant flashes of artillery might have been mistaken for swamp meteors. The show continued for an hour, the advancing and receding fires indicating distinctly the surge of the battle tide. . . . It seemed at length that the fire of the enemy's line began to extend and thicken, while ours wavered and fell back. . . . Between eight and nine o'clock it ceased entirely. . . .

Brigadier General John Gibbon, shown in this wartime portrait, saw it close up as commander of the famed Iron Brigade, which distinguished itself in an engagement against Stonewall Jackson at Groveton during the battle and suffered 33 percent casualties. Gibbon was twice seriously wounded, at Fredericksburg and at Gettysburg. After Appomattox, he fought in the Indian wars, led the relief column at Little Big Horn, and buried George Armstrong Custer and his command.

Captain Alcibades De Blanc [left], aged forty-two when this photograph was taken in the summer of 1862, commanded the outfit he raised, Company C, 8th Louisiana Infantry. He is seen with the company's first lieutenant, twenty-four-year-old Robert S. Perry. De Blanc was promoted to major in September 1862 and lieutenant colonel in April of the following year. He was captured on May 4, 1863, during the Chancellorsville campaign, but was paroled on May 18. He was wounded so severely at Gettysburg that he retired into the invalid corps. Robert S. Perry had enlisted as a private in Company C in June 1861, was elected junior second lieutenant in September, and became De Blanc's adjutant—and a first lieutenant—in May 1862. He was captured on November 7, 1863.

Louisiana soldiers were a breed apart from the rest of the Confederate Army, as Allen C. Redwood discovered when, in the chaos of Second Manassas, he wandered away from his Virginia outfit and ended up among a battalion of Louisianians:

The command was as unlike my own as it was possible to conceive. Such a congress of nations only the cosmopolitan Crescent City could have sent forth, and the tongues of Babel seemed resurrected in its speech. English, German, French, and Spanish, all were represented, to say nothing of Doric brogue and local "gumbo." There was, moreover, a vehemence of utterance and gesture curiously at variance with the reticence of our Virginians.

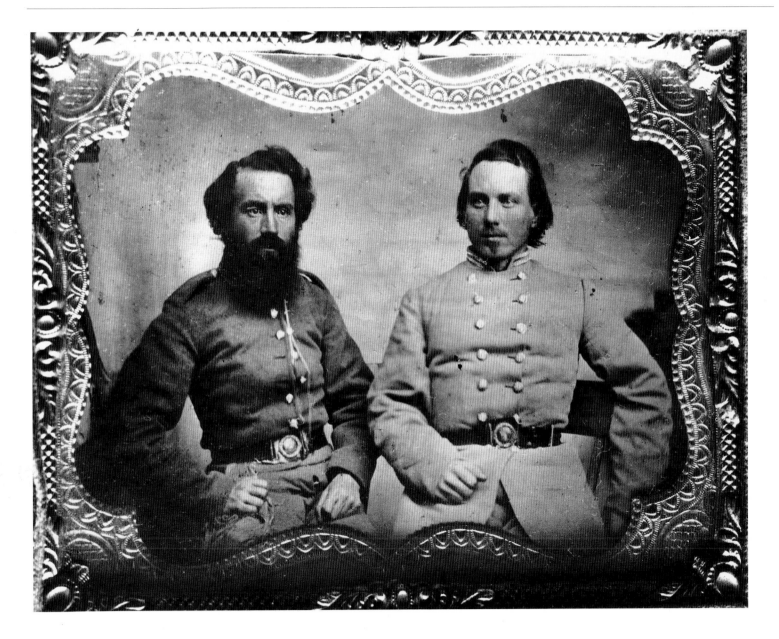

Sister Mary Joseph was a Sister of Mercy, a member of a nursing order that served at the Federal military hospital in Union-occupied Beaufort, South Carolina. Nurses daily witnessed horrors such as an anonymous survivor of Second Manassas describes:

There were six of us . . . and we six had had seven legs amputated. Our condition was horrible in the extreme. Several of us were as innocent of clothing as the hour we were born. Between our mangled bodies and the rough surface of the board floor there was a thin rubber blanket. . . . There were plenty of flies to pester us and irritate our wounds. Our bodies became afflicted with loathsome sores, and—horror indescribable!—maggots found lodgings in wounds and sores, and we were helpless.

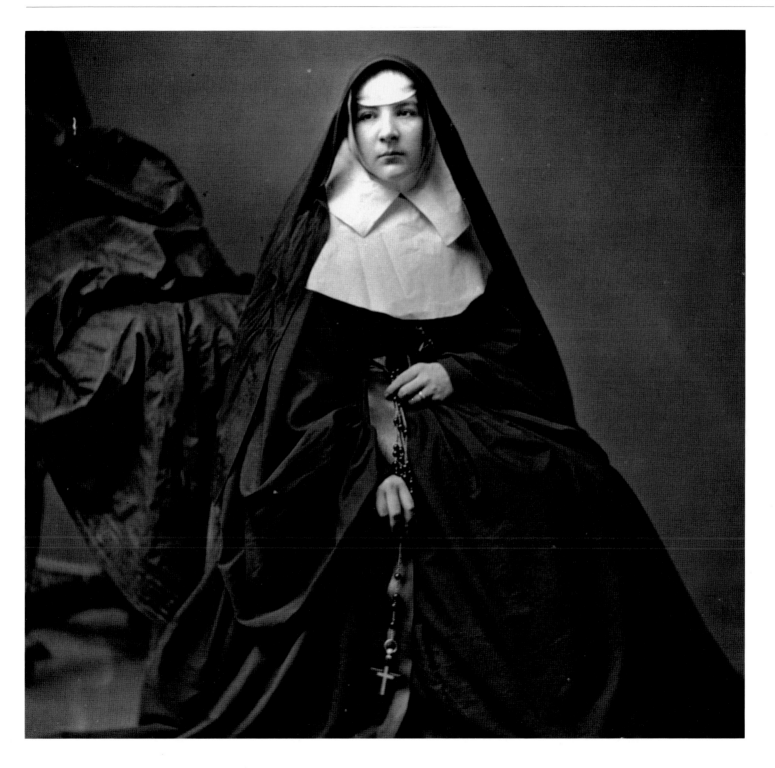

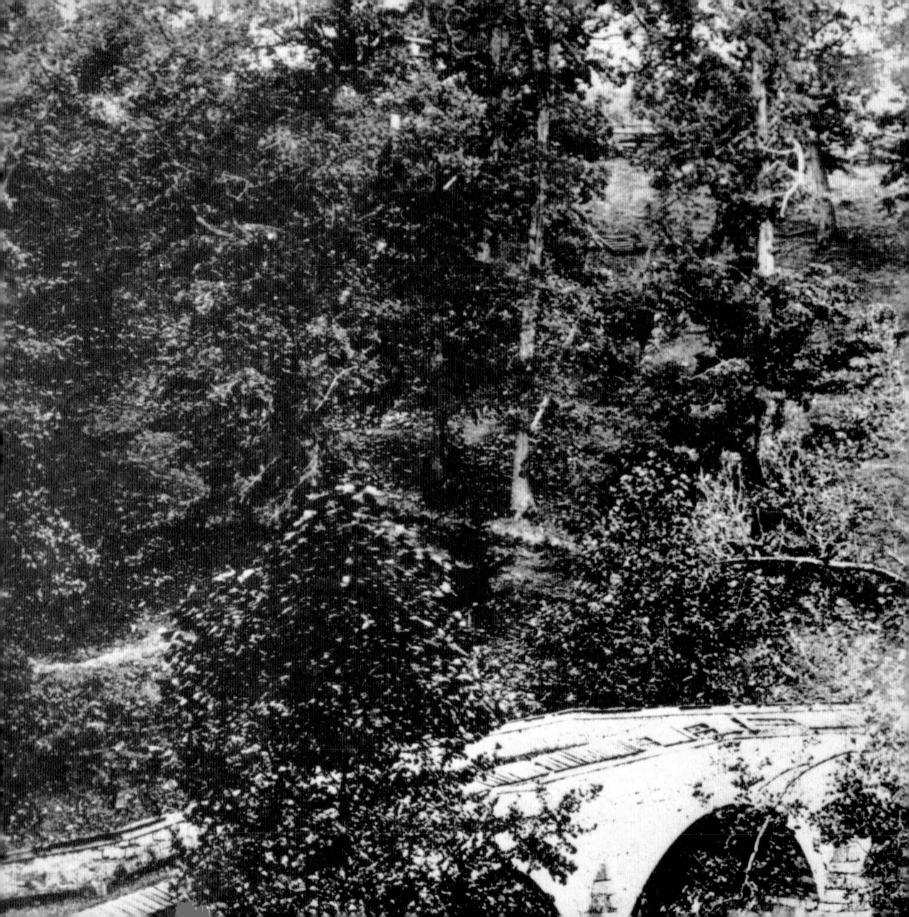

ANTIETAM

September 17, 1862

In early September of 1862, Robert E. Lee invaded the United States of America. He had driven McClellan from Southern soil and now hoped by attacking Maryland to persuade the British to recognize the Confederacy. At the same time, President Abraham Lincoln badly needed a victory in order to emancipate the slaves without it seeming a desperate act against a hitherto victorious South. After several weeks of marching, outgunned, outmanned, and overextended, Lee was on the verge of calling off the invasion, when Stonewall Jackson announced he had taken the Federal arsenal at Harpers Ferry. Lee came to a halt at Sharpsburg and turned to face McClellan.

At Antietam Creek the fighting was some of the hardest of the war, perhaps because it was one of the few battles in which both commanders chose the field and planned their tactics. At dawn on September 17, Union General Joseph "Fighting Joe" Hooker led the attack, coming out of the north down Hagerstown Pike. He drove back Stonewall Jackson's brigade so far, so quickly, that Lee was forced to order up reserves. D. H. Hill's and James Longstreet's Rebels joined the battle in the woods and the cornfields around a church belonging to a pacifist sect called the Dunkers or Dunkards. In late morning, a Yankee division broke through the Confederate line, only to be destroyed in a surprise counterattack by troops just arrived from Harpers Ferry. At midday, the fighting came to center on a sunken farm road called ever afterward "Bloody Lane."

The very weight of Union forces finally drove the Rebels back to the outskirts of Sharpsburg, but McClellan failed to press his advantage and send in his reserves. By nightfall an eerie silence had fallen on the center of the battlefield.

In the late afternoon, Union troops under Major General Ambrose B. Burnside tried to take the only bridge across the Antietam, which was within Rebel rifle range, while Brigadier General Robert A. Toombs's Georgians, hiding behind trees and stone walls, used them for target practice. The photograph shows the bridge, looking toward the Confederate positions held by the 2nd and 20th Georgia regiments.

When Burnside's battered troops finally established their bridgehead by mid-afternoon, putting the North in a position to cut off a Confederate retreat across the Potomac, McClellan once again refused to commit the essential reserves. Before dusk, yet another Confederate division from Harpers Ferry arrived, led by A. P. Hill, and smashed into Burnside's flank, destroying the North's momentum. On the killing fields, 6,000 lay dead, another 17,000 wounded. With barely 30,000 men left in his entire army, Lee stayed on, as if to taunt McClellan, whose mind seemed an open book to the Rebel commander. When McClellan refused the challenge, Lee and all his men slipped away on the eighteenth.

McClellan had won a costly, if strategically vital victory, but he now seemed reluctant even to give chase to Lee. A much-frustrated Abraham Lincoln sacked his general and freed the slaves.

By comparison with the ragtag forces of the South, the Union Army was magnificently equipped, as exemplified by the cornetist of the 2nd U.S. Cavalry pictured here. Yet Northerners were repeatedly chagrined by the frequency with which the ill-equipped Rebels bested them in battle. A Unionist lady wrote of Lee's army marching through Frederick, Maryland:

I wish, my dearest Minnie, you could have witnessed the transit of the Rebel army through our streets. . . . Their coming was unheralded by any pomp and pageant whatever. . . . Instead came three long dirty columns that kept on in an unceasing flow. I could scarcely believe my eyes.

Was this body of men, moving . . . along with no order, their guns carried in every fashion, no two dressed alike, their officers hardly distinguishable from the privates—were these, I asked myself in amazement, were these dirty, lank, ugly specimens of humanity, with shocks of hair sticking through the holes in their hats, and the dust thick on their dirty faces, the men that had coped and encountered successfully and driven back again and again our splendid legions . . . ?

I must confess, Minnie, that I felt humiliated at the thought that this horde of ragamuffins could set our grand army of the Union at defiance. Why, it seemed as if a single regiment of our gallant boys in blue could drive that dirty crew into the river without any trouble!

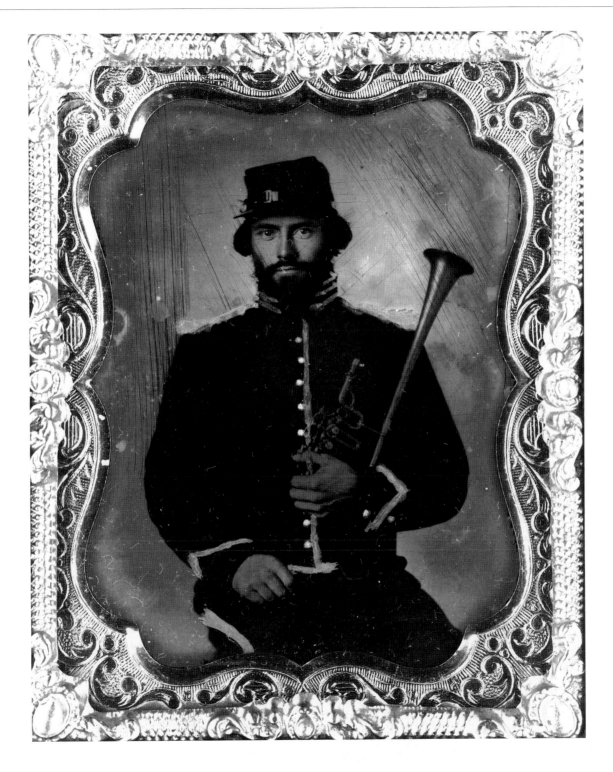

Clara Barton, the future founder of the American Red Cross, volunteered, at her own expense, to nurse the Union wounded in the field. Having cared for the many soldiers wounded at Second Manassas, the "angel of the battlefield" now followed the cannon to Antietam in a hospital wagon she had equipped herself, pausing to gaze down at the encamped army on the eve of battle:

In all this vast assemblage I saw no other trace of woman-kind. I was faint, but could not eat; weary, but could not sleep; depressed, but could not weep. So I climbed into my wagon, tied down the cover, dropped down in the little nook I had occupied so long, and prayed God with all the earnestness of my soul to stay the morrow's strife, or send us victory—and for my poor self—that he impart somewhat of wisdom and strength to my heart—nerve to my arm—speed to my feet, and fill my hands for the terrible duties of the coming day—and heavy and sad I waited its approach.

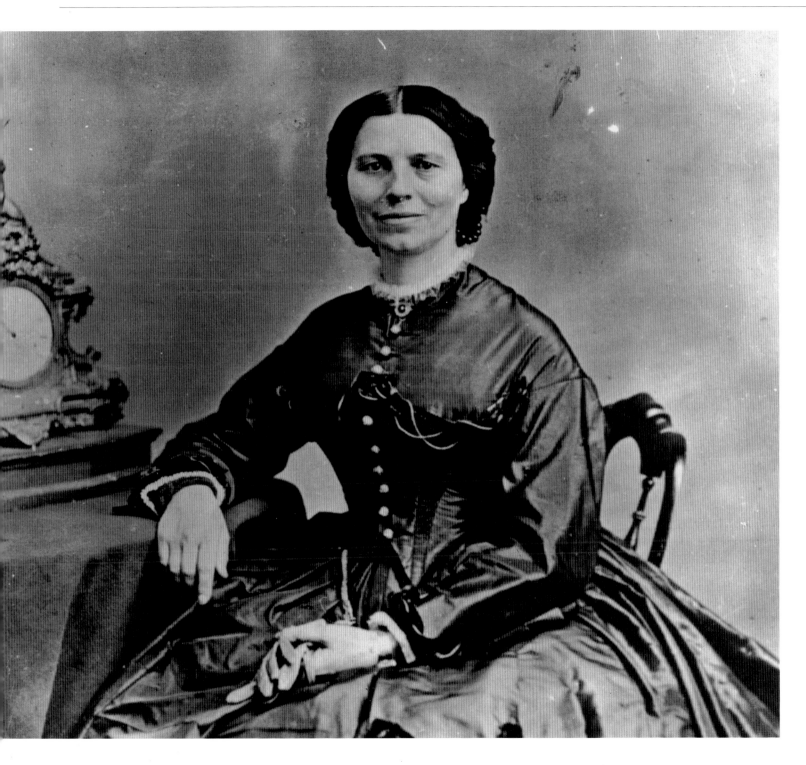

A moment at Antietam, recorded by Alexander Hunter, private, 17th Virginia Infantry:

Our brigade was a mere outline of its former strength, not a sixth remaining. Our regiment, the Seventeenth, that once carried into battle eight hundred muskets, now stood on the crest, ready to die in a forlorn hope, with but forty-six muskets. My company, which often used to march in a grand review in two platoons of fifty men each, carried into Sharpsburg but two muskets (the writer and one other), commanded by Lieutenant Perry. Is it a wonder that we deliberately made up our minds to die on that hill, knowing what a force must be sent against us?

The Confederate soldier in this photograph, identified only as Captain Brow of the 14th North Carolina Regiment, fought in the Battle of Antietam's infamous Bloody Lane.

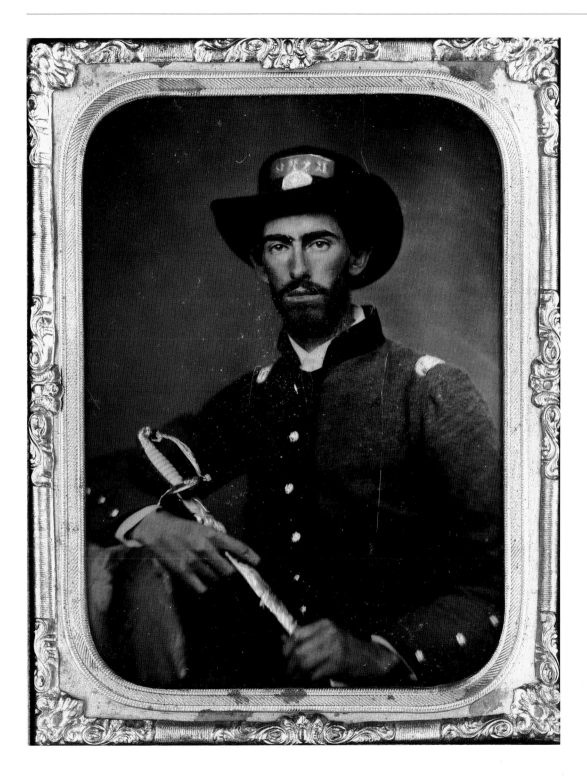

After the humiliation of First Manassas, the Union had looked to thirty-five-year-old George B. McClellan (shown here with his wife and confidante, Ellen Marcy McClellan) as the "Young Napoleon" who would bring swift and decisive victory. A fine administrator and a commander idolized by his men, McClellan proved to be an overcautious disappointment. Lincoln said the general had a bad case of "the slows" and relieved him first as General-in-Chief of the Union armies and then as commander of the Army of the Potomac, after he failed to pursue Lee following Antietam.

Dispatch from McClellan to Major General Henry W. Halleck, September 8: *I am by no means satisfied yet that the enemy has crossed the river in any large force. Our information is still entirely too indefinite to justify definite action. . . . As soon as I find out where to strike, I will be after them without an hour's delay.*

Telegram from McClellan to his wife, September 15: *Have just learned that the enemy are retreating in a panic and our victory complete.*

Dispatch from McClellan to Halleck, September 16: *This morning a heavy fog has thus far prevented us doing more than to ascertain that some of the enemy are still there. Do not know in what force. Will attack as soon as situation of enemy is developed.*

Dispatch from McClellan to Halleck, "September 17, 1862—1.20 P.M.": *We are in the midst of the most terrible battle of the war—perhaps of history. Thus far it looks well, but I have great odds against me. Hurry up all the troops possible. Our loss has been terrific, but we have gained much ground. . . . It will be either a great defeat or a most glorious victory. I think & hope that God will give us a glorious victory.*

Letter from McClellan to his wife, September 18: *The spectacle yesterday was the grandest I could conceive of . . . . Those in whose judgment I rely tell me that I fought the battle splendidly and that it was a masterpiece of art.*

Dispatch from McClellan to Halleck, September 19: *The enemy is driven back into Virginia. Maryland and Pennsylvania are now safe.*

Letter from McClellan to his wife, September 19: *I have the satisfaction of knowing that God has, in His mercy, a second time made me the instrument for saving the nation.*

On October 25, McClellan forwarded to Halleck a report from one of his cavalry officers: *"Our mounts are absolutely broken down from fatigue and want of flesh."* Citing this, McClellan protested that, despite Halleck's and Lincoln's urging, he could not pursue Lee's forces to Richmond until he received fresh horses and supplies.

Telegram from President Abraham Lincoln in response to McClellan's October 25 dispatch to Halleck: *Will you pardon me for asking what the horses of your army have done since the battle of Antietam that fatigues anything?*

Order from Lincoln to Halleck, November 5: *By direction of the President, it is ordered that Major General McClellan be relieved from the command of the Army of the Potomac; and that Major General Burnside take the command of that Army.*

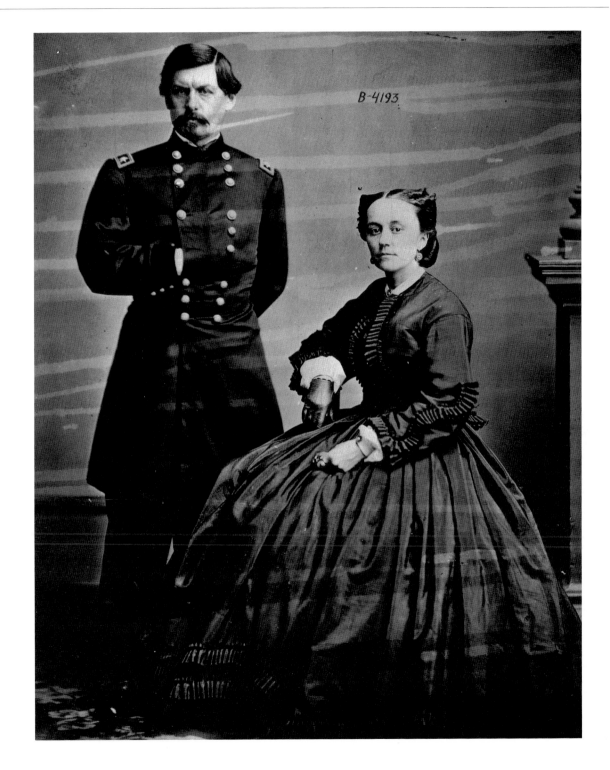

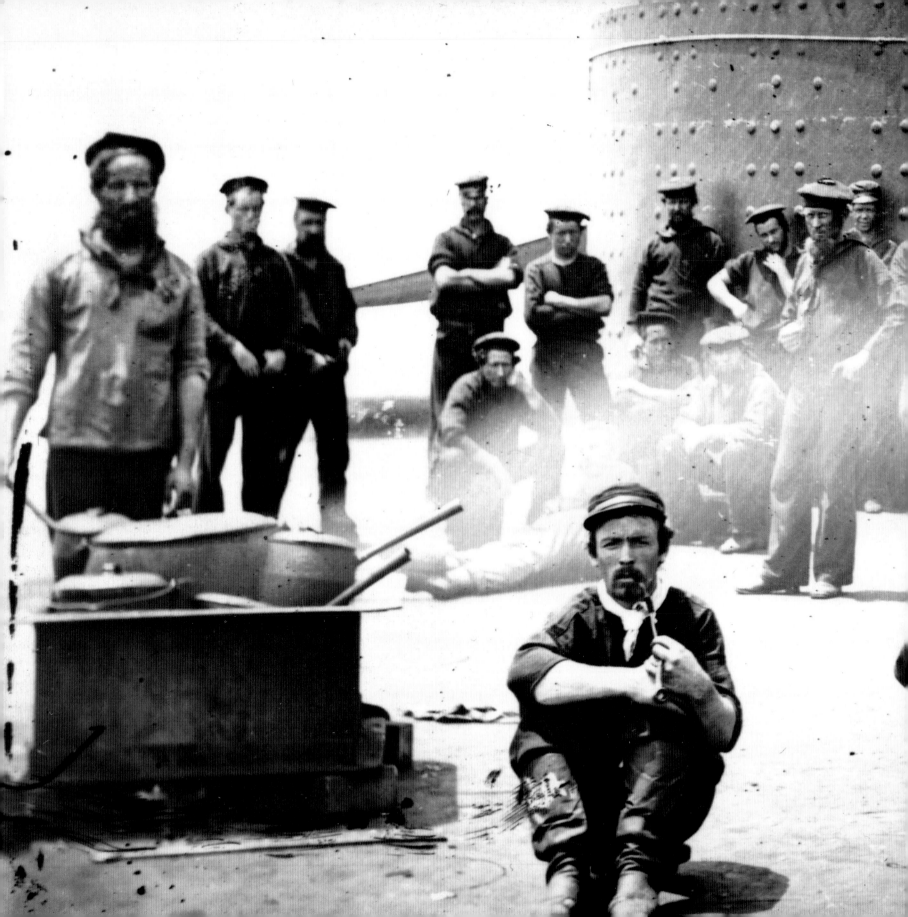

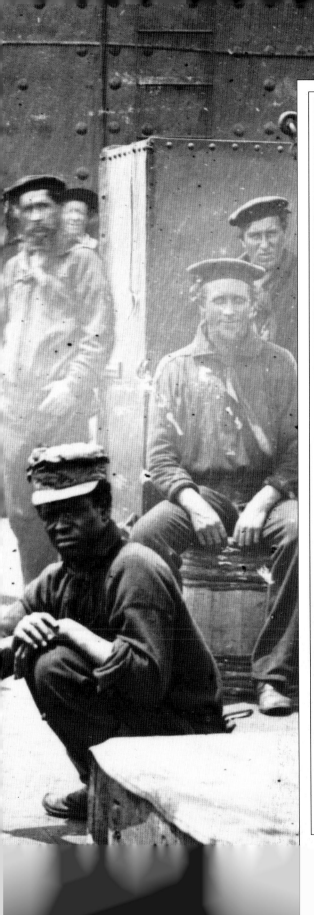

THE *MONITOR, MERRIMACK,* AND TWO NAVIES

When Abraham Lincoln became president, most of the forty-two seaworthy ships of the ninety vessels comprising the U.S. Navy patrolled waters thousands of miles from the shores of America. But the North had a large merchant marine from which to cull experienced officers and sailors and boasted nearly all of the country's shipbuilding capacity. Under the leadership of gray-bearded Gideon Welles (whom Lincoln called "Father Neptune") and his dynamic assistant, Gustavus V. Fox, the Union Navy, within weeks of Lincoln's declaration of a blockade against Rebel ports on April 19, 1861, had commissioned scores of merchant ships, armed them well, and dispatched them south. By the end of the year, the Union had more than 250 warships at its command and 100 more under construction.

The Confederate States of America began the Civil War without a navy, but by the fall of 1861, the Confederacy had managed to build a small fleet of new ships that were the harbingers of a revolution in naval warfare. The first of these to see significant action had once been a steam frigate called the *Merrimack,* scuttled by the U.S. Navy when it abandoned Norfolk. Refitted with iron plates bolted together on its hull and upper structure and rechristened the *C.S.S. Virginia,* she first saw action on March 8. That morning she steamed to attack the Union fleet blockading the Virginia coast out of Hampton Roads. The shells of the fifty-gun *U.S.S. Cumberland,* the North's most potent conventional frigate, bounced off the new ironclad "like India rubber balls" as the Confederate warship rammed her and sank her in shallow water. In short order, the Rebel boat set the *Congress* on fire and drove the *Minnesota* aground. For a single day, the South ruled the sea.

But next morning, when the Confederate ironclad headed for the helpless *Minnesota* to finish her off, its crew came upon a strange looking craft made entirely of iron and lying, more awkwardly than menacingly, in wait for them. It was the *U.S.S Monitor,* commissioned by a panic-stricken Union Navy from the irascible Swedish-born inventor John Ericsson. Already in a dispute with the federal government over payment for past service, Ericsson could barely be persuaded to build the craft. It had trundled out of New York harbor some six weeks earlier, leaking water and spewing gas as it limped southward, arriving just in time.

Sporting a unique revolving gun-turret—the canvas-covered structure in the background of the photograph—which would become the hallmark of modern battleships, the *Monitor* proved its worth against the Confederate monster. Union Navy Lieutenant S. Dana Greene recorded what it was like to fight an iron ship with an iron ship, taking particular note of imperfections in the design of the *Monitor's* revolving turret, which housed two 11-inch, 180-pound, smoothbore Dahlgren guns.

Our shots ripped [into] the iron of the Merrimac, while the reverberation of her shots against the tower caused anything but a pleasant sensation. While Stodder, who was stationed at the machine which controlled the revolving motion of the turret, was incautiously leaning against the side of the tower, a large shot struck in the vicinity and disabled him. He left the turret and went below, and Stimmers, who had assisted him, continued to do the work.

The drawbacks to the position of the pilot-house were soon realized. We could not fire ahead nor within several points of the bow, since the blast from our own guns would have injured the people in the pilot-house, only a few yards off. . . . As the engagement continued, the working of the turret was not altogether satisfactory. It was difficult to start it revolving, or, when once started, to stop it, on account of the imperfections of the novel machinery, which was now undergoing its first trial.

After a four-and-a-half-hour, nose-to-nose battle, the *Virginia*, neé *Merrimack*, finally withdrew. She never again saw action. Two months later, the Rebels—forced in turn to abandon Norfolk—blew her up. As to the *Monitor*, some of its battle-hardened crew

members posed for a photograph in a quieter moment. Note the smoke of the cookstove and the presence of a black crewman, who stoked the fires that fed the vessel's steam engine.

In the aftermath of the ironclads' duel, the Union blockade grew ever more effective. In the beginning, some nine out of ten blockade runners, many of them British operating out of Nassau and Havana, slipped through what Southerners insisted was a mere "paper" blockade. By war's end, one out of two were caught, and the Navy was blockading the Bahamas and Cuba—over loud protests from other nations—as well as the Confederate coast.

It was the U.S. Navy, under sixty-year-old, Tennessee-born Admiral David G. Farragut, that captured New Orleans early in April of 1862. The South, outgunned at sea, became adept at mining its harbors with what were then called "torpedoes." The Confederate Navy also initiated submarine warfare. In an attempt to alleviate the pressure of the blockade at Charleston, it launched a crude underwater vessel named the *Hunley*, whose inventor and thirteen others drowned in the course of three test runs. After each disaster, the vessel was refloated, and finally, its single screw cranked by hand, a mine strapped to a spar projecting out from its bow, the *Hunley* slipped into the harbor and blew up the Union steamer *Housatonic*, only to be sunk itself for a fourth and final time in the resulting explosion. All hands aboard the *Hunley* were lost; most of the *Housatonic's* crew were rescued.

When Farragut led a Union flotilla of eighteen ships to close Mobile and tighten the Union blockade even further in July of 1864, his lead ship sank when it hit a Confederate mine. Farragut, suffering from vertigo so severe he ordered himself lashed to the rigging of his flagship, thundered "Damn the torpedoes, full speed ahead!" Bouncing off waterlogged mines that failed to detonate, Farragut's flotilla took the port.

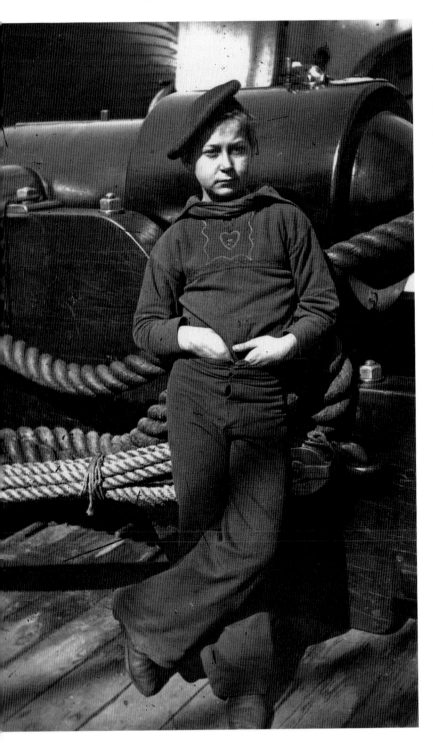

Nineteenth-century warships customarily counted among their gunnery crews boys known as powder monkeys, like this lad on the *U.S.S. New Hampshire.* The boys, valued for their agility, ran from gun to gun, delivering powder, shot, water, and the like. Baptized by fire, they grew up fast—if they survived. John C. Kinney, an army signal officer assigned to the service of Union Admiral David Farragut aboard the *U.S.S. Hartford*, recalled what it was like to come under attack:

Owing to the Hartford's *position, only her few bow guns could be used, while a deadly rain of shot and shell was falling on her, and her men were being cut down by scores, unable to make reply. The sight on deck was sickening beyond the power of words to portray. Shot after shot came through the side, mowing down the men, deluging the decks with blood, and scattering mangled fragments of humanity so thickly that it was difficult to stand on the deck, so slippery was it.*

Raphael Semmes, legendary Confederate naval commander, captured eighteen vessels in six months while skipper of the *Sumter*, and sixty-nine vessels as captain of the *Alabama*. Before the Civil War, he was an officer of the United States Navy, but resigned his commission when his adoptive state, Alabama, seceded from the Union. His letter of resignation, addressed to Secretary of the Navy Isaac Toucey, suggests much about the man's character:

Washington, D.C.
February 15th 1861

Sir:

I respectfully tender, through you, to the President of the United States, this, my resignation of the commission, which I have the honor to hold, as a Commander in the Navy of the United States.

In severing my connection with the government of the United States, and with the Department over which you preside, I pray you to accept my thanks, for the kindness which has characterized your official deportment towards me.

I have the honor to be
Very respectfully
Your Obt. Svt.

Raphael Semmes
Commder U.S. Navy

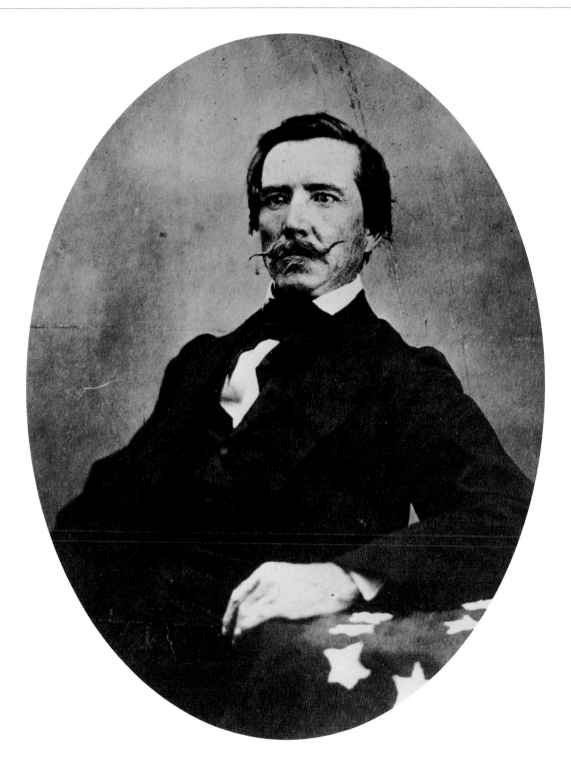

FREDERICKSBURG

December 11–13, 1862

After Lincoln sacked McClellan for good, he turned his army over to Ambrose Burnside, who—determined to be the aggressive general for whom his president longed—immediately marched south through a cold rain toward Richmond with 120,000 grumbling troops. In late November, he reached a line of hills overlooking Fredericksburg, Virginia. The bridges across the Rappahannock River had been destroyed, like the one photographed here in April 1863 by Union Captain A. J. Russell. The figures on the far side are soldiers of Barksdale's Mississippi Brigade, which saw heavy fighting at Fredericksburg. (It is said that this is the only wartime picture of Confederate soldiers taken by a Union photographer.)

With the bridges out, Burnside was forced to wait for the arrival of pontoon bridges to cross the Rappahannock and take the town. By the time they arrived seventeen days later, Robert E. Lee had entrenched 75,000 troops in a six-and-one-half-mile line along the crest of the hills.

On December 11, the Federal forces began shelling Fredericksburg, setting much of the town on fire. Against what seemed token resistance, the Union soldiers crossed the river on six pontoon bridges under cover of their artillery and fought house-to-house, dodging Rebel snipers, to take the town, which they thoroughly and wantonly looted. Burnside, believing that Lee expected him to cross the river either above or below Fredericksburg, had opted for a frontal assault. Lee, hardly believing his good fortune, had only lightly defended the town in order to reinforce Longstreet's men along the crest of Marye's Heights in anticipation of Burnside's straight-ahead attack.

The result, as one Union general had warned Burnside, was "murder, not warfare." On the other side, as one of Longstreet's artillery officers put it, "a chicken could not live on that field when we open on it."

The assault came in two parts on December 13. Union General William Franklin attacked Jackson on the left, while the main force under "Fighting Joe" Hooker attempted to storm the heavily fortified Marye's Heights. Fourteen charges later, some 13,000 Union troops lay dead, dying, or wounded, as many as at the killing fields of Antietam. Some, trapped on the battlefield all night, froze to death. Others, still alive the next day, tried not to hear the smack of Rebel bullets into the wall of corpses behind which they hid. A distraught, weeping Burnside announced he would lead a new attack himself. Persuaded instead to withdraw back across the river, he heard his aide call for three cheers as he rode past his men. The response was absolute silence.

Back in Fredericksburg, a member of Stonewall Jackson's staff, surveying the devastation visited by the Yankees, asked his general what sort of men would do these things.

"Kill 'em," Jackson replied. "Kill 'em all."

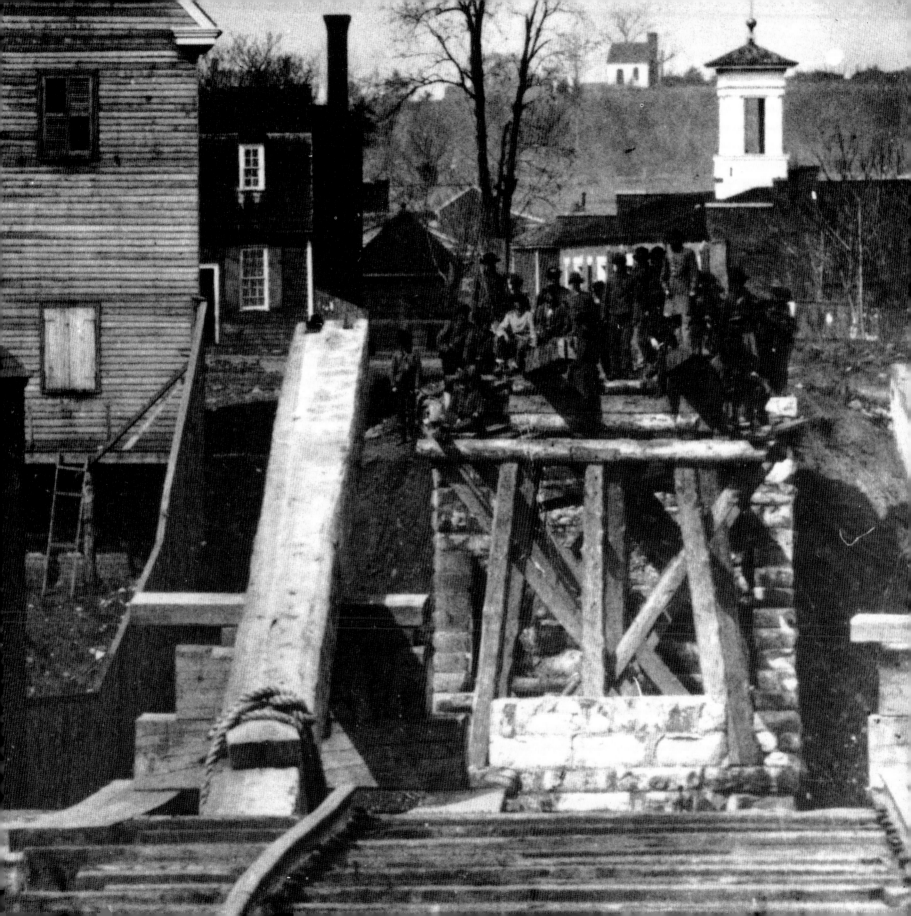

Not surprisingly, Civil War memoirs and letters abound in descriptions of wounded men. The widespread use of newly developed forms of artillery, which sent murderous shell fragments in every direction, inflicted head injuries, often with grotesque results, as in this instance at Fredericksburg:

I saw one man with gun in hand, walking with a firm step and a cheerful countenance, having been struck by a piece of shell in the forehead, laying bare the brain so I could see every pulsation.

Bathed in such carnage, one wonders why Union photographer Captain A. J. Russell had this Zouave *pose* as a wounded soldier. As it is, the photo is not very convincing. The Zouave, most likely a member of the spit-and-polish 5th New York, has managed miraculously to keep his spanking-white gaiters spotless and his modern 1861 Springfield rifle musket in equally pristine condition.

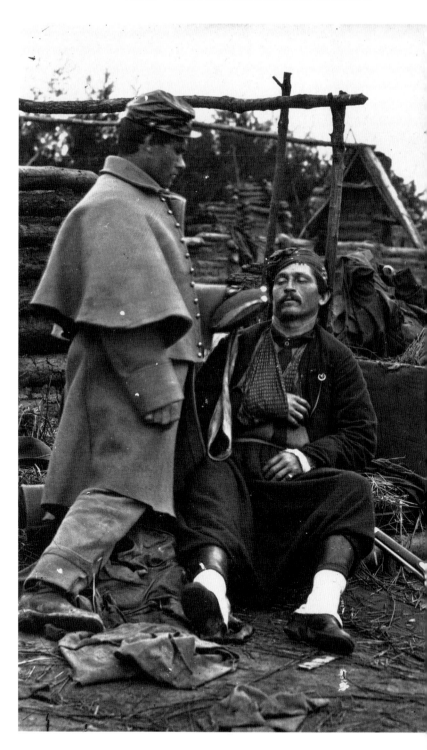

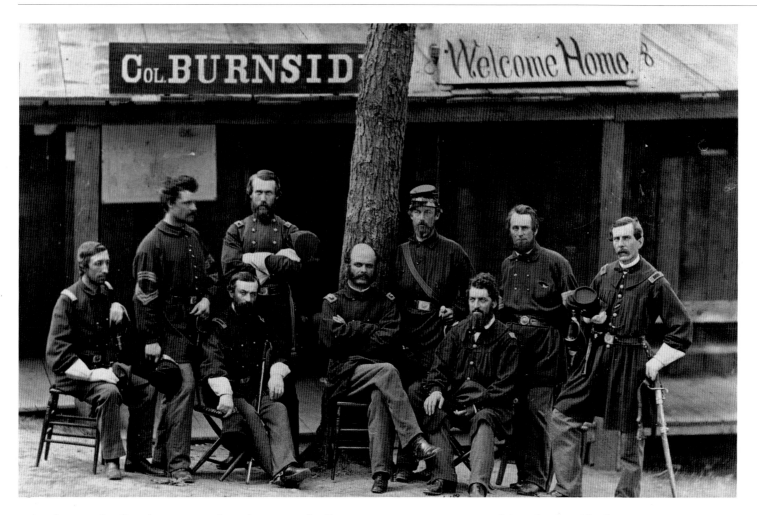

A photograph of Ambrose Burnside and regimental officers at the outbreak of the war, when he was the popular colonel of the 1st Rhode Island Volunteers. After removing George B. McClellan as commander of the Army of the Potomac, Abraham Lincoln twice offered the post to Burnside, who twice declined it. He was persuaded to accept after a third offer, led his command to defeat at Fredericksburg, and was replaced by "Fighting Joe" Hooker. "Gone are the proud hopes," William Thompson Lusk wrote in a war letter to his mother, which was published years later:

. . . the high aspirations that swelled our bosoms a few days ago.

Once more unsuccessful, and only a bloody record to show our men were brave. . . . [The army] has strong limbs to march and meet the foe, stout arms to strike heavy blows, brave hearts to dare—but the brains, the brains! Have we no brains to use the arms and limbs and eager hearts with cunning? Perhaps Old Abe has some funny story to tell appropriate to the occasion.

Ulysses S. Grant was equally direct but more judicious in his assessment of Burnside, calling him "an officer who was generally liked and respected. He was not, however, fitted to command an army. No one knew this better than himself."

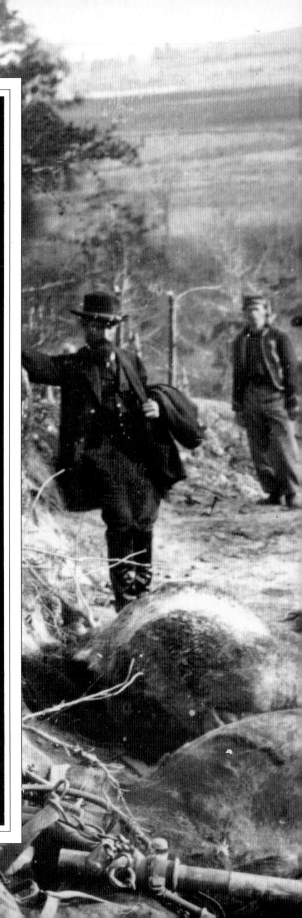

CHANCELLORSVILLE

May 2–4, 1863

When "Fighting Joe" Hooker took over the Army of the Potomac from General Ambrose Burnside (who had taken over from George B. McClellan), he had twice as many men as his opponent, Robert E. Lee, whose 60,000 troops stood uneasy guard outside Fredericksburg just across the Rappahannock River from Hooker's position. Boasting that he would show Lee no mercy, Hooker split his force in three. He sent 10,000 cavalry far upstream to cut the Rebel supply lines. Another 70,000 infantry headed upriver to attack Lee's left, camping on the night of April 30 outside Chancellorsville. Hooker ordered his 40,000 remaining troops to feign an advance on Fredericksburg to keep Lee in place until the flanking attack was under way.

Lee, with his typical tactical acumen, did not take the bait. Guessing correctly that the main threat lay in Chancellorsville, he left a mere 10,000 infantry under Colonel Jubal Early to hold Fredericksburg and marched the rest into battle on May 1. Hooker ordered his superior force to withdraw to defensive positions around the little Virginia crossroads. The next day, Lee split his troops again, sending Jackson and 30,000 foot soldiers—screened by "Jeb" Stuart's cavalry—on a daring flanking maneuver across the enemy's front while holding his line against Hooker's main force with only 15,000 men. The battle lasted for two more days, until Hooker—seemingly mesmerized by Lee into never employing more than half his force at any one time—decided to retreat across the river. It had been yet another remarkable but costly Southern victory. While the Union had lost 17,000 men to Lee's 13,000, the figures represented only 17 percent of Hooker's army compared to nearly one-fourth of the Confederate forces. Among the 13,000 had been Stonewall Jackson, Lee's strong right arm, shot accidently by his own pickets.

The photograph shows that horses as well as men became casualties of war. Brigadier General Herman Haupt (left), Chief of Construction and Transportation, U.S. Military Railroads, gazes at the blasted wreck of what had been part of an artillery battery. This is another photograph by Captain Andrew J. Russell, who, detailed to Haupt's staff, set up his own photographic department.

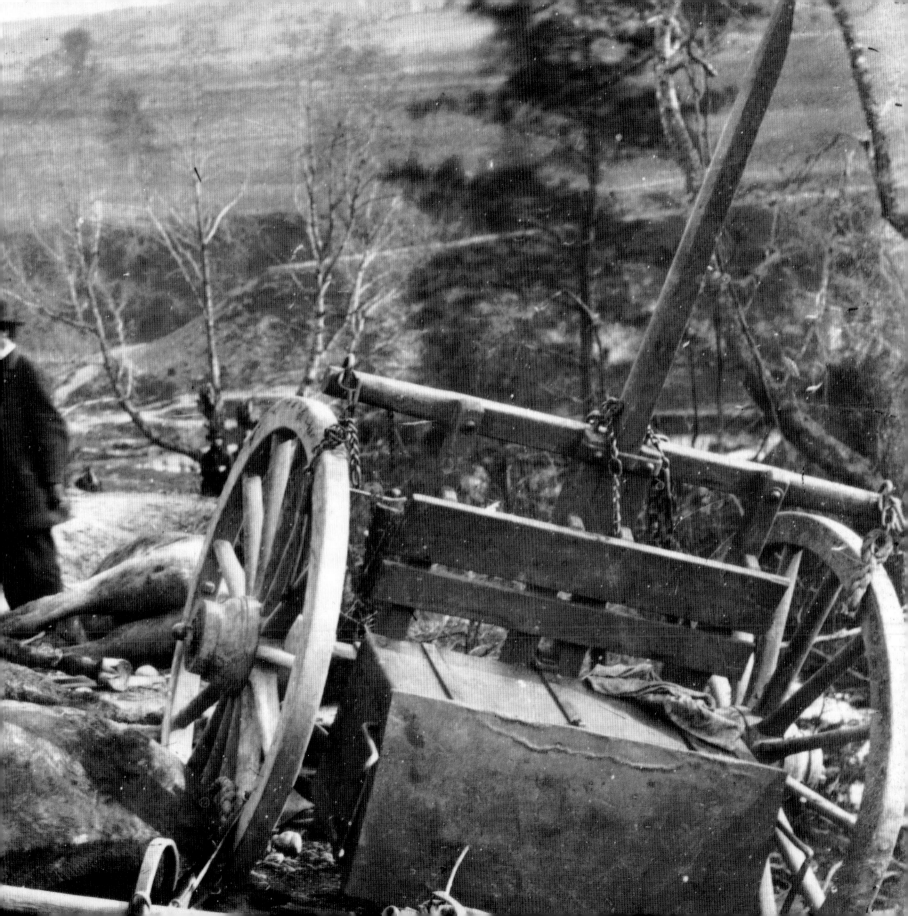

Southerners had no cause to complain about their leadership at Chancellorsville, not with commanders like Lieutenant General Thomas J. ("Stonewall") Jackson in charge. Then the unthinkable happened. While organizing his forces for a night attack, Jackson was accidentally fired upon by his own men. He was hit in the right hand, left wrist and hand, and left arm. Although none of the wounds was in itself mortal, pneumonia set in and felled him. He died on May 10, as his physician, Dr. Hunter McGuire, relates:

His mind . . . began to . . . wander, and he frequently talked as if in command upon the field . . . .

About half-past one he was told that he had but two hours to live, and he answered . . . feebly but firmly, "Very good; it is all right."

A few moments before he died he cried out in his delirium, "Order A. P. Hill to prepare for action! Pass the infantry to the front rapidly. Tell Major Hawks—" then stopped, leaving the sentence unfinished.

Presently a smile . . . spread itself over his pale face, and he said quietly, and with an expression as if of relief, "Let us cross over the river and rest under the shade of the trees."

This photograph, Jackson's last, was taken three or four months before his death.

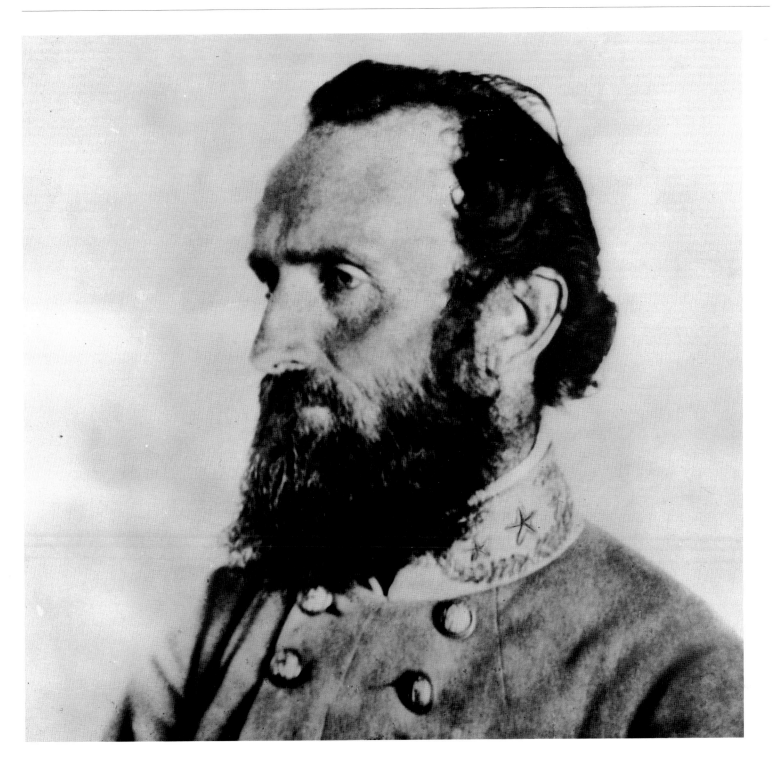

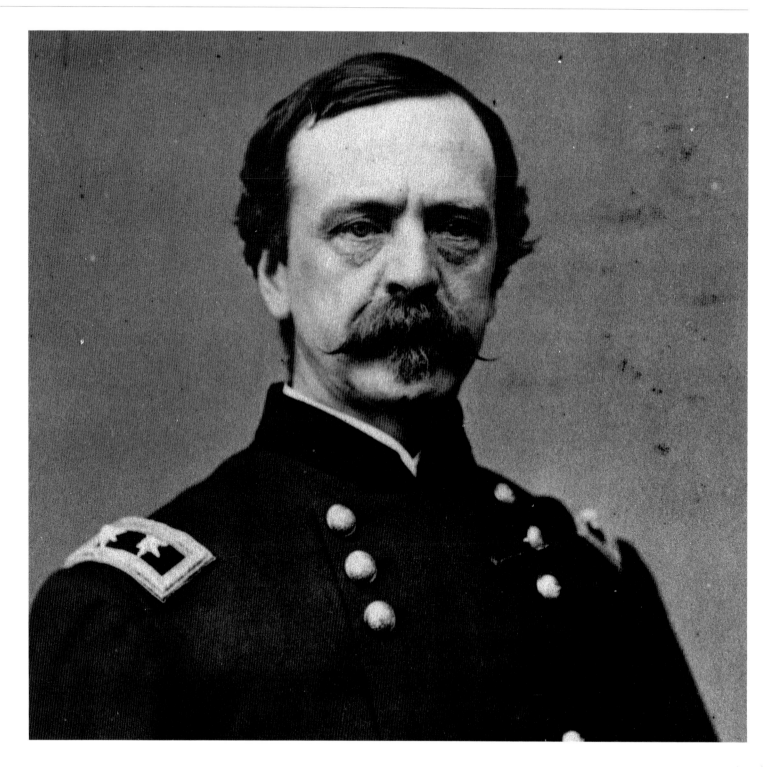

Union Brigadier (later Major) General Daniel Edgar Sickles could not approach Lee or Jackson for military genius, but the war produced few figures possessed of more audacity and productive of more controversy. Two years before the start of the war, in Lafayette Park—just across Pennsylvania Avenue from the White House—Sickles shot and killed Philip Barton Key (son of "Star-Spangled Banner" lyricist Francis Scott Key), who had allegedly been sleeping with his wife. Tried for murder, Sickles, for the first time in legal history, pleaded not guilty by reason of temporary insanity. He was acquitted. That was scandalous enough; he created further shock waves by taking his errant wife back to hearth, home, and bed.

At the outbreak of war, he raised the Excelsior brigade of New York City and was commissioned colonel of the 20th New York, one of five regiments in the brigade. Abraham Lincoln, a close friend, nominated him for brigadier general in September of 1861, but the Senate rejected the nomination. A second nomination was approved. Sickles commanded troops at Williamsburg, Fair Oaks, and Malvern Hills during the Peninsular Campaign, and at Antietam, Fredericksburg, Chancellorsville, and Gettysburg, where he lost a leg to a Rebel cannonball but picked up the newly created Congressional Medal of Honor.

The crippled general remained in active service, though not in combat, carrying out a secret diplomatic mission to South America and serving as military governor of the Carolinas. President Andrew Johnson, disturbed by the zeal with which Sickles performed the work of Reconstruction, removed him from the Carolinas in 1867. In 1869, he became U.S. minister to Spain but resigned amid scandal in 1873. Named chairman of the New York State Monuments Commission in 1886, he was dismissed in 1912 for mishandling funds. He died, embittered and defiant, in 1914, aged eighty-nine.

Dissension and controversy surrounded Sickles, but one thing nobody argued about was his appetite for a good time. Agnes Leclerque, a Baltimorean who had starred in the circus as a trick rider before marrying Austrian Prince Felix de Salm-Salm (who immigrated to the United States and became colonel of the 8th New York), recalled the festivities at an encampment near Washington in the winter of 1863:

. . . I especially remember [a party] given by General Sickles, in a hall improvised from canvas by uniting a dozen or more large hospital tents in a convenient manner.

This immense tent was decorated inside and outside with flags, garlands, flowers and Chinese lamps in great profusion, and offered a fairy-like aspect. The supper laid under the tent for about two hundred persons, ladies and gentlemen, could not have been better in Paris, for the famous Delmonico from New York had come himself to superintend the repast, and brought with him his kitchen aides and batteries, and immense quantities of the choicest provisions and delicacies, together with plate and silver, and whatever was required to make one forget that it was a camp supper. The wines and liquors were in correspondence with the rest, and no less, I suppose, the bill to be paid.

"We lead the *dullest imaginable* life here," a soldier wrote to his fiancée about the boredom of a winter camp. Even the dingiest of winter soldier shacks were, however, graced with (generally ironic) names: Pine Cottage, Uncle Tom's Cabin, Hawkins's Happy Family, Fifth Avenue Hotel, Social Circle, Mess of Cabbage, Old Abe's Parlor, Chateau de Salt Junk, San Souci, Buzzard's Roost, Swine Hotel, Yahoos, Rest for the Pilgrims, Hole in the Wall, Potpourri, Devil's Inn, The House That Jack Built, and We're Out. Breaking the boredom at "Pine Cottage"—a Union winter encampment, probably near Washington, D.C.—a corporal plies a whisk broom on the frock coat of his sergeant; the man in the doorway has a bite to eat; another blacks his shoes, while a comrade-at-arms tells him how to go about it. The woodcutter and the wielder of the broom execute their functions indifferently at best. On the roof, a private prepares to drop something on his sergeant or the man in the doorway, who, like the three men to his left, wears a "smoking cap," a colorful non-regulation item fashionable for off-duty hours in camp.

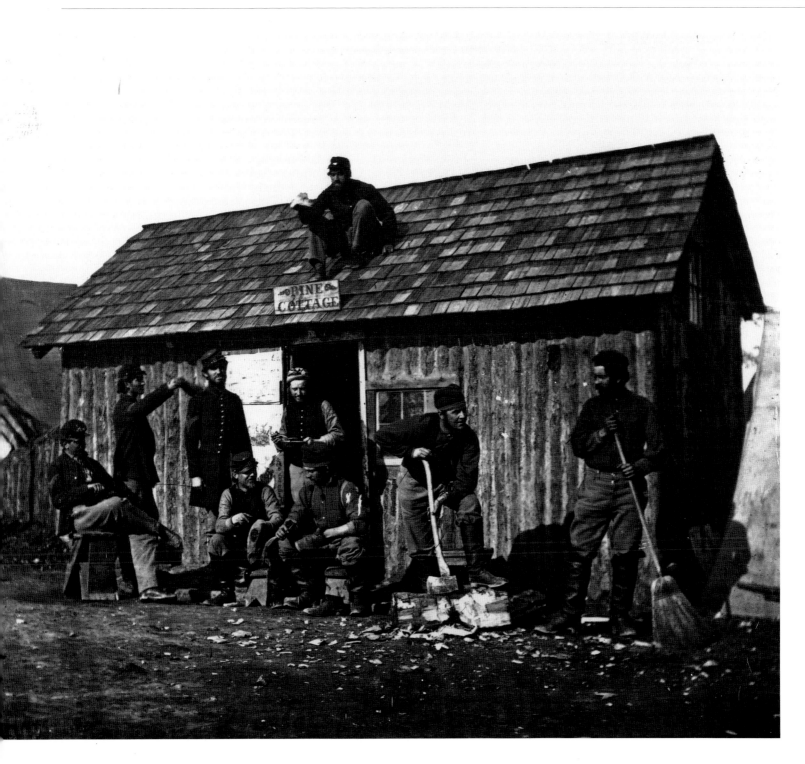

VICKSBURG

October 1862–July 4, 1863

After the battle of Corinth in October of 1862, Ulysses S. Grant headed south along the Mississippi Central Railroad to take Vicksburg, which sat high on a bluff four hundred miles north of New Orleans, blocking Union control of the Mississippi. From his forward base at Holly Springs, Grant managed to advance his 40,000 troops to Oxford by December, before he ran up against the 20,000 men that John C. Pemberton, in charge of Vicksburg's defense, had entrenched along the Yalabusha River. Nathan Bedford Forrest, his cavalry augmented by guerrillas, attacked Grant's exposed supply line, destroying much of the 150 miles of railroad in Grant's rear and forcing him to withdraw. Sherman had been advancing downriver from Memphis as Grant invaded overland. Unable to communicate with his commander, Sherman assumed Grant would be occupying Pemberton's troops and launched an assault on the Vicksburg bluffs, only to have his men mowed down like tin targets in a shooting gallery.

Bolstered by the failure of Grant's winter campaign, Pemberton assumed the Yankees were scampering back to Memphis and sent most of his cavalry—and, in early spring, some 8,000 infantry as well—to help out Braxton Bragg in Tennessee. Grant, who had learned in his retreat that his soldiers did not need a supply line, but could survive by foraging, now boldly turned his army and marched it down the west bank of the Mississippi to a point below Vicksburg. He ordered the Union fleet to run the gauntlet of the Vicksburg batteries for a rendezvous. Floating downriver

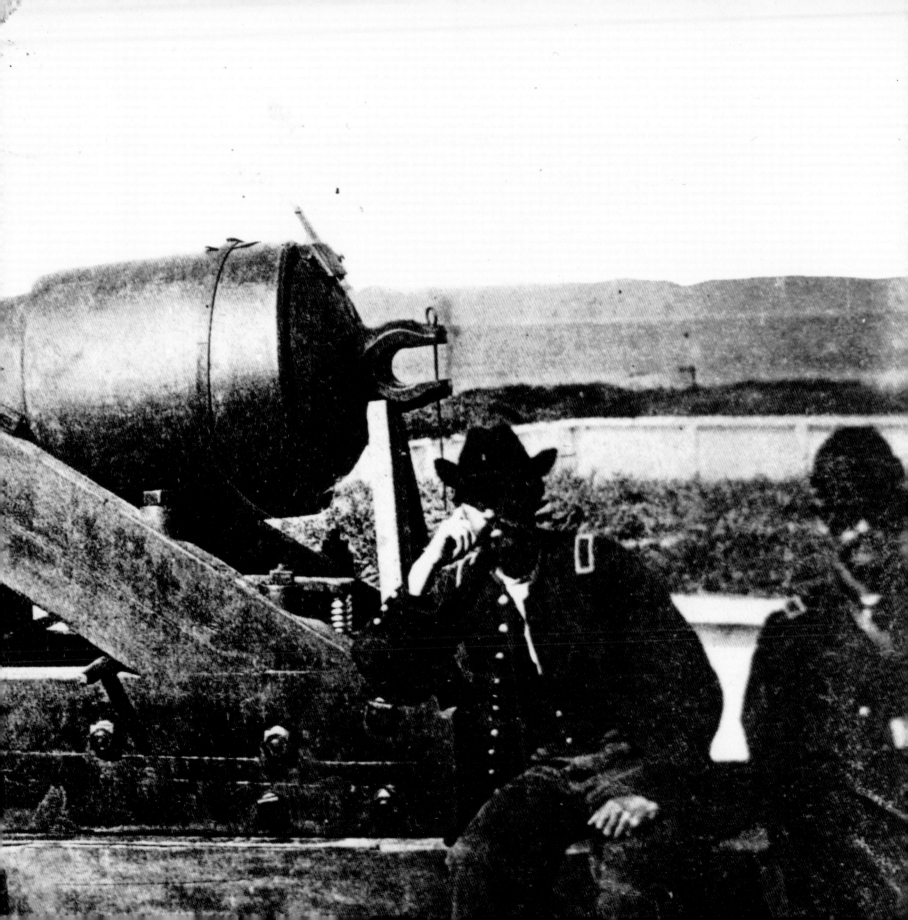

silently on moonless nights in April, most of the gunboats got through even though Rebel sentries spotted them from time to time, and Vicksburg's gunners shelled them by the light of hastily built bonfires along the banks. Among the guns used against the Union fleet was the one pictured here, "Whistling Dick," the most famous gun of the Civil War. On May 27, 1864, this Confederate 18-pounder sank the Union gunboat *Cincinnati*. Originally a smoothbore manufactured at Richmond's Tredegar Iron Works, Whistling Dick was subsequently rifled in such a way that projectiles fired from it were launched with a characteristic spin that produced a whistling noise. Hence the nickname.

Thirty miles south of the Confederate's vaunted "Gibralter of the West," Grant's army met the Union fleet and crossed the Mississippi. Then, instead of heading straight for his target, Grant launched a seventeen-day campaign to destroy all Rebel forces in the area that might attack his flanks during an assault on the town. When he finally marched on Vicksburg, his confident troops eagerly charged the maze of trenches, rifle pits, and artillery, only to suffer the fate of Sherman's troops six months earlier in the hail of fire pouring down on them. By May 24, Grant had settled in for a siege.

As more than 200 Union guns pounded Vicksburg every day, its denizens dug caves in the yellow-clay hillsides and outfitted them with furniture brought from home. Weeks dragged by, full of suspense, terror, and boredom, while Grant slowly, inexorably tightened the noose. Vicksburg's civilians grew lice-ridden and despondent, were reduced to eating mules, horses, dogs, and took to tearing down fences and houses for firewood. By July it was clear that the reinforcements the local paper had been promising from General Bragg were not coming, and on July 4, Pemberton surrendered. When the Union troops marched into town, there was scarcely a taunt from the half-starved crowds that met them, and the soldiers not only shared their rations with the civilians, but broke into the stores held by certain "speculators" and threw the "luxuries" into the streets for anyone to eat.

Victory at Vicksburg cut the South in half and secured the Mississippi River for the North. Coming simultaneously with Gettysburg, it marked the turning point of the struggle and was therefore the most important Northern strategic victory of the war, a victory that the town commemorated for some eighty-one years afterward by refusing to celebrate the Fourth of July.

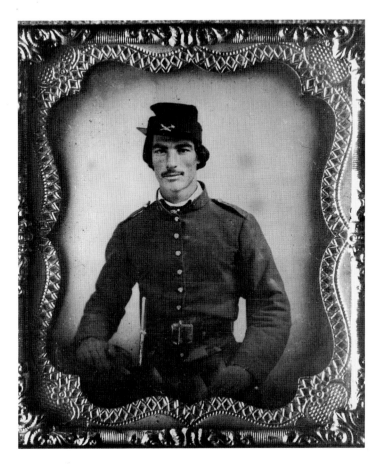

Fisher, bastion on the Cape Fear River, North Carolina, recorded the execution, for desertion, of privates Vincent Allen and Dempsey Watts of the 36th North Carolina Artillery:

Thursday Nov 24th, 1864

25 min. after 11 o'clk, the prisoners left Maj. Stevenson's office in the ambulance accompanied by Chaplain McKinnon. They were guarded by the reserve of eight men under a corporal. The officer of Guard & Surgeons accompanied the guard. The battalion was drawn up in two lines facing the prisoners. Light Artillery & Scouts [on the] right. Infantry battalion under Capt. Munn [on the] left.

Prisoners arriving at stakes, a prayer was offered by Chaplain. They declined making any remarks and requested not to be tied. They knelt down facing the guard & were blindfolded. There were nine men for each condemned man, one squad under the sergeant and the other under Officer Guard.

At the command "aim," one file fired. The officer of the Guard immediately followed with command "fire," but the discharge was irregular. Allen, who was at the old stake, was instantly killed. Watts was only wounded, but mortally. He groaned distressingly, "Lord have mercy on me," when I immediately ordered up the reserve of four to within two paces of him & he received two shots through the head, & died. Both men were cool, Watts as calm as if he had been on parade, the last thing he did before being blindfolded, was to turn and look at Allen & adjust his arms & hands like his. Allen stood during the Chaplain's prayer & seemed a little affected but as if in prayer. He was praying while shot.

After execution, the troops were broke into columns & marched around the bodies to the dead march. The bodies were carried to Camp Wyatt.

Confederate Sergeant Joseph Cornielle originally served in the 22nd Louisiana Infantry, which was subsequently reorganized as the 23rd Louisiana Infantry or Artillery. Cornielle deserted on July 16, 1863, shortly after the fall of Vicksburg, and was held in the North as a POW until the end of the war. Languishing in the starvation and squalor of a prison camp was bad enough, but the consequences of desertion could have been worse. By the end of the war, one out of every ten Federals had deserted, as had one of seven Confederates—a total of 420,000 soldiers North and South. Both sides attempted to control the epidemic of desertions by meting out capital punishment at summary court-martials. Colonel William Lamb, commandant at Confederate Fort

GETTYSBURG

July 1–3, 1863

On June 30, Lieutenant General A. P. Hill's corps of Confederates was marching toward Gettysburg, Pennsylvania, in search of shoes, a commodity always in short supply. Union Brigadier General John Buford's cavalry division engaged Hill two miles outside of town, while other Confederate and Union forces converged on the sleepy village that commanded an important crossroads. The first day of battle went badly for the Union. Hill's troops killed Major General John F. Reynolds, commander of the Union I Corps, almost as soon as he came onto the field. Reynolds's veterans held their ground and were reinforced by Major General Oliver O. Howard's XI Corps. In the afternoon, however, a joint attack by Hill and Lieutenant General R. S. Ewell drove the Federals through the town in disarray. On Cemetery Hill, the Union soldiers rallied, took up a new position, and were augmented by fresh troops arriving from the south and east. The Confederates took up an encircling position, part of which occupied Seminary Ridge, parallel to Cemetery Ridge.

Robert E. Lee attacked on July 2, failed to achieve a double envelopment of the Union forces, but did inflict very heavy losses. On July 3, Lee ordered a direct attack—across open country—on the Union's center. Fifteen thousand Confederate troops advanced against the Union position on Cemetery Ridge. The Southerners withered under heavy artillery and musket fire, except for a small number of determined men, including Major General George Pickett's division, the only fresh troops in the attack. Pickett's forces suffered badly: two brigadiers were killed, the third severely wounded, and all fifteen of Pickett's regimental commanders were killed or wounded. At the Angle, 150 men led by Brigadier General Lewis Armistead briefly raised the Confederate colors above Cemetery Ridge—but the men were soon cut down or captured.

The 93rd New York Volunteer Infantry was one of many units that fought at Gettysburg. Its drum corps was photographed at Bealton, Virginia, in August 1863, a month after the battle. Only two of the soldiers wear the regulation musician's coat with piping across the chest, and the complement is an odd mix of boys and men—with a *boy* bearing the baton and sash of chief musician.

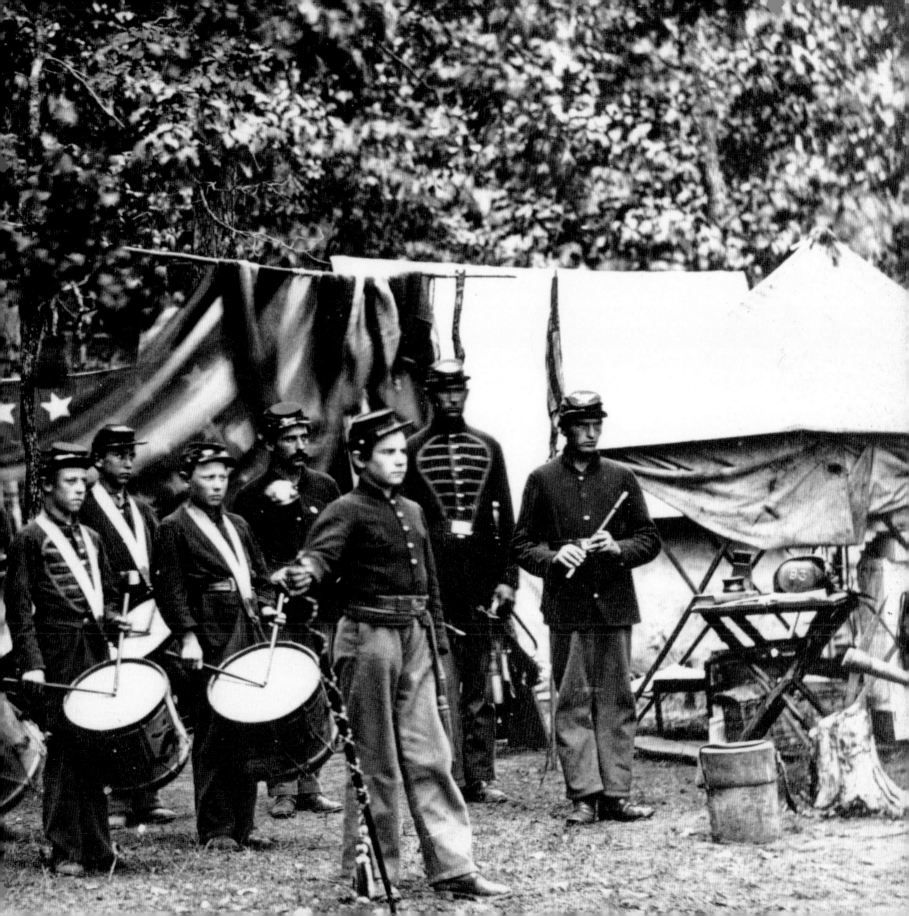

Private Ira Fish, 150th New York Infantry, was among the approximately 28,000 soldiers, North and South, wounded at Gettysburg. "I remember," wrote one of Confederate Lieutenant General James Longstreet's officers:

. . . one with the most horrible wound that I ever saw. We were halted for a moment by a fence, and as the men threw it down for the guns to pass, I saw in one of the corners a man sitting down and looking up at me. A solid shot had carried away both jaws and his tongue. I noticed the powder smut from the shot on the white skin around the wound. He sat up and looked at me steadily, and I looked at him until the guns could pass; but nothing, of course, could be done for him.

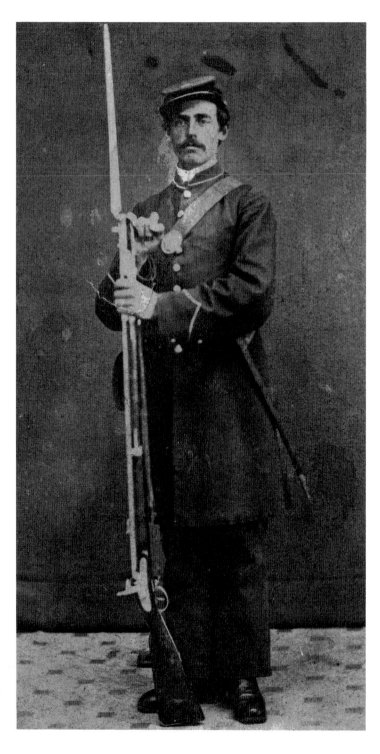

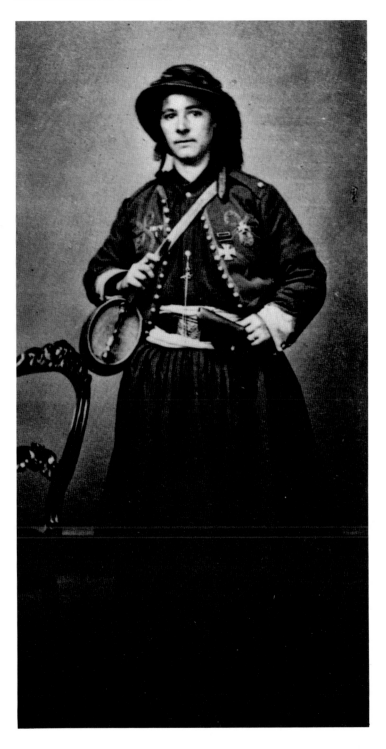

"French Mary" Tepe was a *vivandière* who served with the 114th Pennsylvania Volunteers, Collis's Zouaves. The tradition of such female attendants to the regiment—combination nurses and sutlers—goes back to the Thirty Years' War in Europe. A few Civil War regiments adopted the custom, especially in organizations primarily made up of foreign-born men. A female presence was, understandably, sorely missed by men at war. Camp followers—prostitutes—there were in plenty, and some were downright ingenious; the Washington provost marshal's office regularly arrested women who had disguised themselves as men in order to march undetected with the regiment. But men whose youth had been rudely interrupted missed the tenderness of a mother or a sweetheart. One recent scholar, James I. Robertson, Jr., quotes an unpublished letter from Virginia cavalryman Andy Crockett to a friend:

I must tell you a secret. down on the Jeems River the other day I saw a—a—gal, that is a lady. right thar, I lost my heart, as well as the little bit of sense I had   Ef I could get that gal, I'd give anything that I've got. Yes! I'd even part with my new red cotton Handkerchief.

Illinois soldier John Shank sent this to the folks back home:

I wrote a letter to my sweet Hart—one that i intend to Have for my Wedded Wief if i ever get Home Safe again. she is Bout 16 years old. She had Black Eyes and dark Hair and fair skin and plenty of land and that hant all.

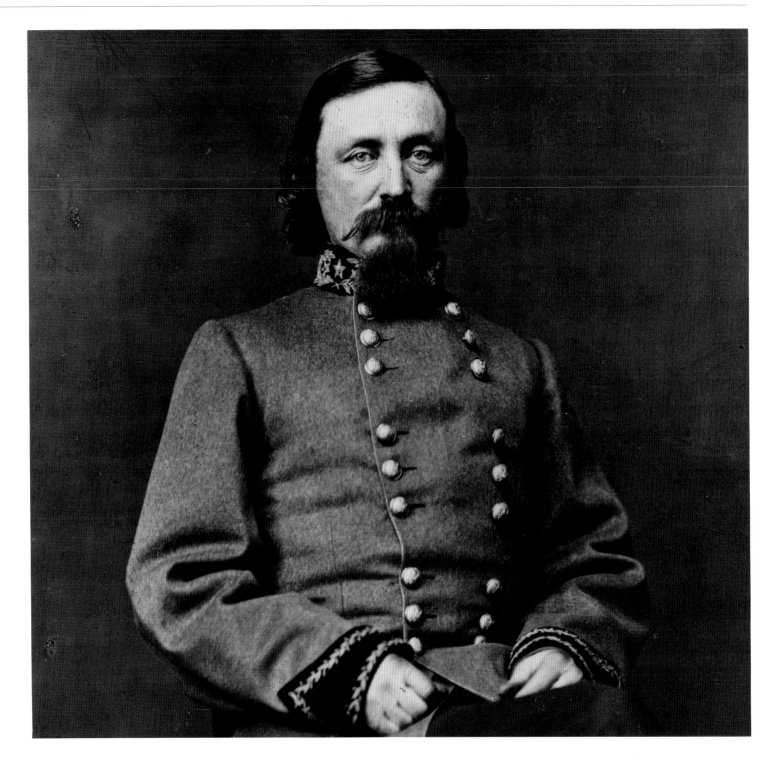

On July 3, Major General George Pickett led a daring, desperate, futile, and instantly celebrated charge against the Union position on the all-too-aptly named Cemetery Ridge. That night, Pickett wrote to his fiancée:

My brave boys were so full of hope and confident of victory as I led them forth! Over on Cemetery Ridge the Federals beheld a scene which has never previously been enacted—an army forming in line of battle in full view, under their very eyes—charging across a space nearly a mile in length, pride and glory soon to be crushed by an overwhelming heartbreak.

Well, it is all over now. The awful rain of shot and shell was a sob—a gasp.

I can still hear them cheering as I gave the order, "Forward!" the thrill of their joyous voices as they called out, "We'll follow you, Marse George, we'll follow you!" On, how faithfully they followed me on—on—to their death, and I led them on—on—on—Oh God!

I can't write you a love letter today, my Sally. But for you, my darling, I would rather, a million times rather, sleep in an unknown grave.

Your sorrowing
Soldier

These Confederate prisoners taken at Gettysburg look more like jaunty figures out of American folklore than examples of a defeated enemy. Short of men, short of provisions, short of arms and ammunition, the Southern army was long on spirit. General John B. Gordon, who commanded a Georgia brigade at Gettysburg (and elsewhere), tells of riding with General Richard S. Ewell:

. . . through the streets of Gettysburg. In a previous battle [Groveton, at Second Manassas] he had lost one of his legs, but prided himself on the efficiency of the wooden one which he used in its place. As we rode together, a body of Union soldiers, posted behind some buildings and fences on the outskirts of the town, suddenly opened a brisk fire. A number of Confederates were killed or wounded, and I heard the ominous thud of a Minie ball as it struck General Ewell, at my side.

I quickly asked, "Are you hurt, sir?"

"No, no," he replied, "I'm not hurt. . . . It don't hurt a bit to be shot in a wooden leg."

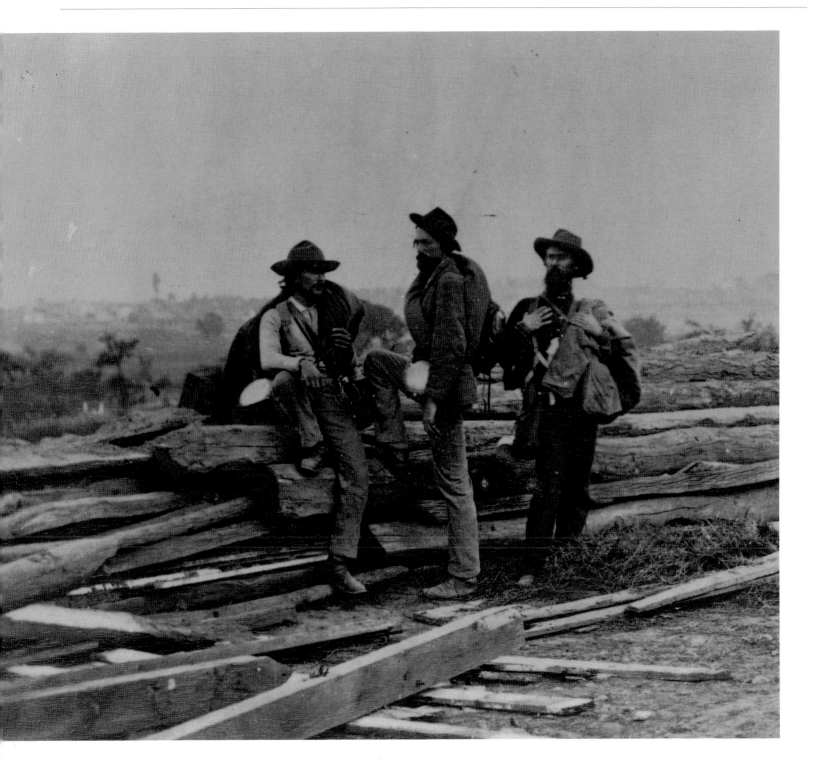

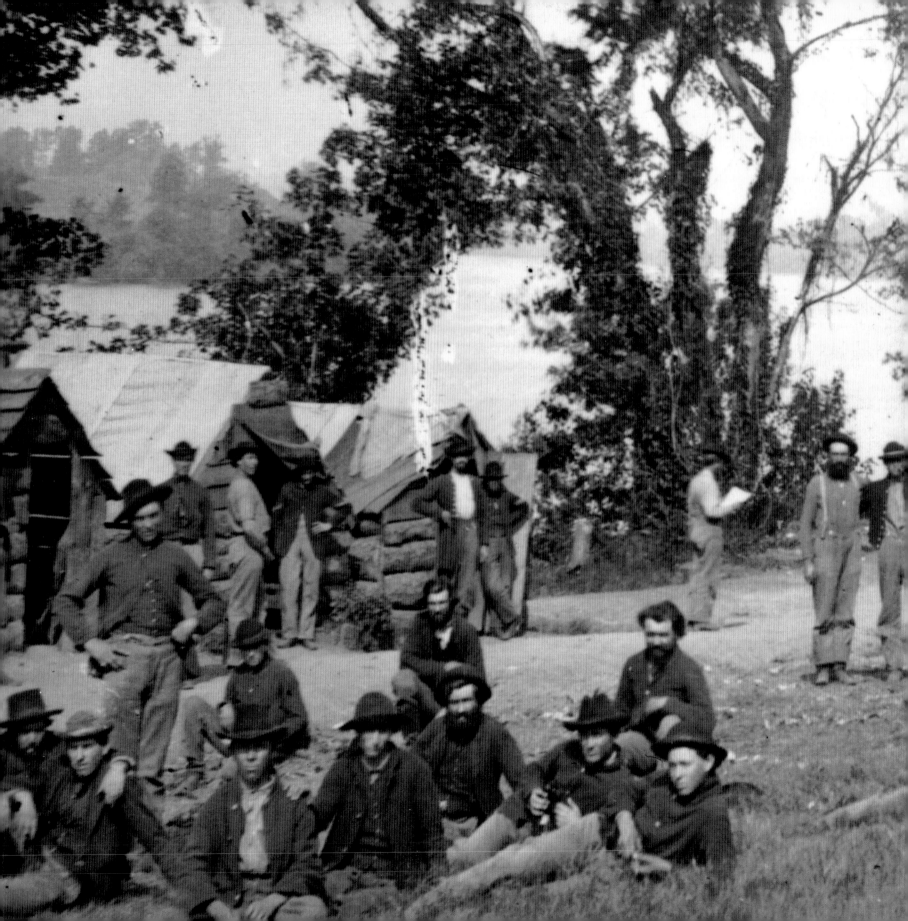

CHICKAMAUGA AND CHATTANOOGA

September 19–20, 1863
November 23–25, 1863

For half a year, General William "Old Rosy" Rosecrans—head of the Union's Army of the Cumberland—had dallied with Braxton Bragg's Army of Tennessee without ever engaging in anything like a real battle. When Lincoln threatened dismissal in June, Rosecrans finally struck in a series of quick, nearly bloodless flanking maneuvers that drove Bragg eighty miles east across middle Tennessee in little more than a week. There matters came more or less to a halt. Still, by September, Rosecrans was installed in Chattanooga, and Bragg had to be reinforced by 12,000 Virginia troops under General James Longstreet.

On September 19, a now more aggressive Bragg lured part of the Union army out of the city and attacked it along Chickamauga Creek in the bloodiest battle of the western theater. After two days of brutal fighting, Rosecrans blundered mightily by ordering his troops to close what he thought was a gap in his line. The gap did not, in fact, exist, and the attempt to fill it only opened up a real one. Longstreet stormed through and routed the Yankees. Only two things saved Rosecrans from destruction: Bragg failed to follow up his advantage, and Union General Henry Thomas at the last minute mounted a stubborn, staged withdrawal, earning him the nickname "the Rock of Chickamauga." The heated two-day battle cost 4,000 lives and nearly 35,000 other casualties, including Rosecrans's job.

As General Ulysses S. Grant was rushed in to take charge of the miserable, cold, lice-infested, ill-supplied, and demoralized troops bottled up in Chattanooga, the Southern command fell to bickering. Braxton Bragg, a Louisiana sugar planter equally despised by common foot soldier and fellow officer, was reviled by Longstreet and Bedford Forrest for his inaction at Chickamauga. Ultimately, Confederate President Jefferson Davis had to visit Bragg's headquarters personally to settle the dispute—unpopularly, enough—in Bragg's favor. The South could ill afford such dissension, for Grant was on the move.

He had punched through the Confederate perimeter, built a pontoon bridge across the Tennessee River, established a sixty-mile "cracker line" to feed his troops, and was ready to fight. Bragg's army looked down on Grant's men from the six-mile-long crest of Missionary Ridge east of the city. West and south Confederate guns loomed, massed on the summit of Lookout Mountain, some 2,000 feet high. Grant decided simply to drive the Rebels out of their nests. On November 24, the two-day battle of Chattanooga began.

The first day, William Tecumseh Sherman's attack on the left foundered, but "Fighting Joe" Hooker's men slugged their way up Lookout Mountain through a dense fog to take the summit in the so-called "Battle Above the Clouds." That left the seemingly impregnable Missionary Ridge, its crest bristling with artillery, its slopes pocked with rifle pits, its base fully entrenched. When Hooker's all-out assault faltered the next morning, General Thomas's veterans of Chickamauga, feeling they had something to prove, charged up the middle of the hill, sweeping all before them. A puzzled Grant asked, "Who ordered those men up the hill?" An aide replied, "No one." In the face of this onslaught, 4,000 Rebel troops surrendered. Most of the Confederates simply threw down their guns and ran.

The action at Chickamauga began near Lee & Gordon's Mills, as Federal Private Arthur van Lisle recalled:

On they come, that long gray line, so long that the flanks extend beyond our vision. Steady is their step and perfect their alignment, save here and there as they meet an obstruction in the way of a farmhouse or a fence. There is heard to the right and left some irregular firing and occasional cannon shot, and then for a moment a crash and rumbling like the thunders rolling from cloud to cloud. In our immediate front, however, all is quiet. It is that dread silence that precedes the approaching storm.

On it comes, and now a general shout breaks forth. It is the Rebel yell, "Hey—Yeh—Yeh! Hey—Yeh—Yeh!" They have started on the double-quick toward us. . . . We have witnessed similar demonstrations before and have withstood them. We only clutch our rifles more firmly and brace ourselves to receive the shock. . . . Suddenly they halt. They are probably eighty rods distant . . . and before they have time to adjust themselves in position, or bring their guns from a right-shoulder-shift, we are given the command, "Ready! Aim! Fire!"

A sheet of flame issues from our ranks; a cloud of smoke fills the air and obscures our vision. We reload and await results as we watch the vapor rising from the ground. We see a flash, as of sheet-lightning; we hear the report; we see our comrades falling, some never to rise again, some mortally wounded, weltering in blood, others crippled and writhing in agony.

Now "forward" is the order, and we advance on the enemy, leaving our stricken comrades behind us where they have fallen. The battle is on in earnest. . . .

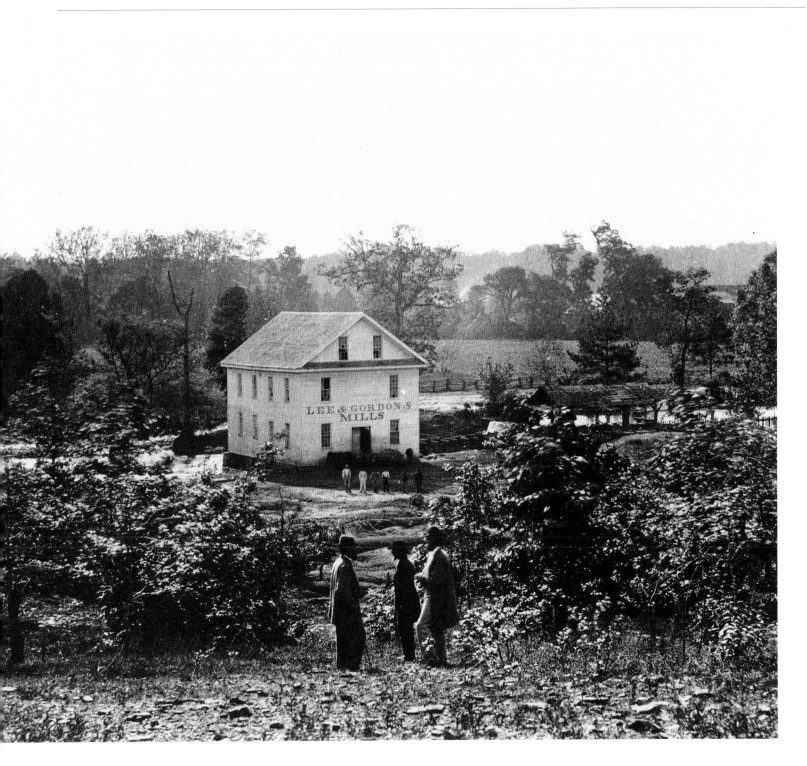

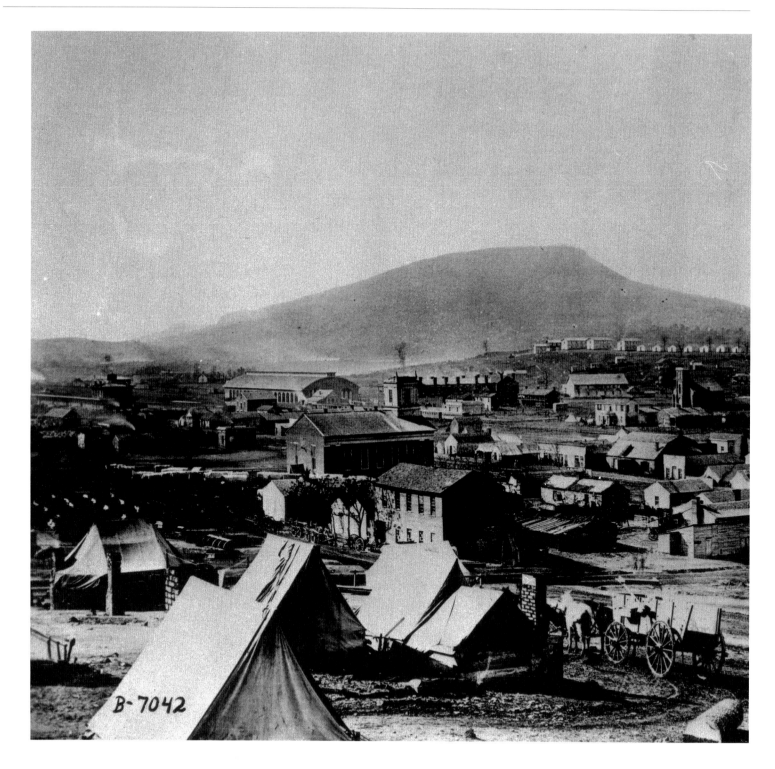

W. F. G. Shanks, a Union war correspondent, described Chattanooga, which is seen here in an 1863 photograph, looking toward Lookout Mountain:

If there was little of beauty or elegance in the place when our troops retreated into it from Chickamauga, there was a great deal less a fortnight subsequently. . . . Residences were turned into blockhouses; black bastions sprang up in former vineyards; rifle pits were run through the graveyards; and soon a long line of works stretched from the river above to the river below the city . . . .

[The] quarters of the troops, composed of small dog-kennel-shaped huts, built of boards and roofed over with the shelter-tents with which the soldiers were provided, were scattered all over the town, in valley and on hillside . . . .

The 60th North Carolina, which James T. Weaver commanded, fought at Chattanooga. In this photograph, the Library of Congress identifies Weaver as a lieutenant colonel. At the time of the battle, he was a major, though he was in command of the regiment. The uniform he wears in this reversed-image ambrotype was probably that of a first lieutenant, Weaver's original rank. The collar insignia for a first lieutenant, two horizontal stripes, has been retouched into a single bar, and gold lace on the sleeves has been added or embellished. Such tokens of rank were important to officers, but made little positive impression on enlisted men tormented by hunger. For during the Confederate siege of Union-held Chattanooga, both sides went hungry. One of the besiegers, Private Sam Watkins, 1st Tennessee, recalled:

Our rations were cooked up by a special detail ten miles in the rear and were sent to us every three days; and then those three days' rations were generally eaten at one meal, and the soldiers had to starve the other two days and a half. The soldiers were . . . almost naked, and covered all over with vermin and camp-itch and filth and dirt. The men looked sick, hollow-eyed, and heart-broken. . . .

In the very acme of our privations and hunger, when the army was most dissatisfied and unhappy, we were ordered into line . . . to be reviewed by the Honorable Jefferson Davis. When he passed us with his great retinue of staff-officers . . . at full gallop, cheers greeted him, with the words, "Send us something to eat, Massa Jeff. I'm hungry! I'm hungry!"

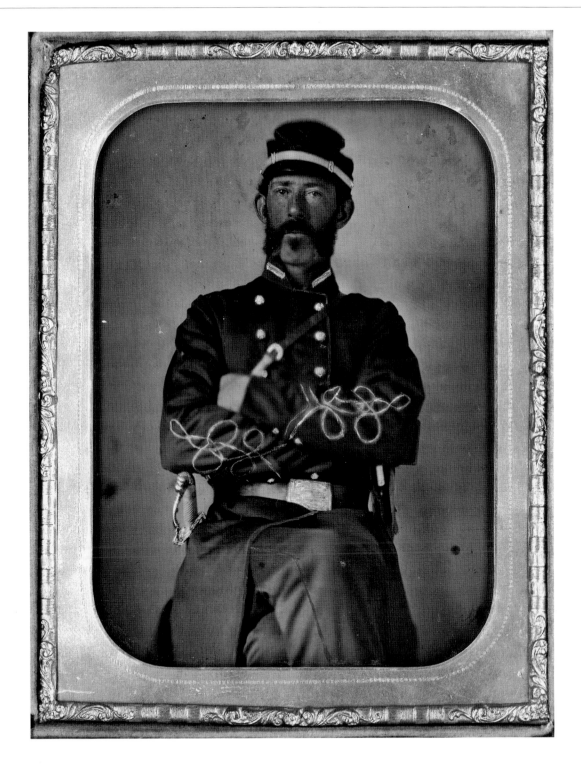

The Union army of occupation "expelled" from Nashville the beautiful Pauline Cushman, an actress of French and Spanish ancestry, calling her a confirmed secessionist. The expulsion constituted sufficient patriotic reason for Confederate officers to seek her company. Indeed, they found the lady irresistible both for her political views and her physical charms. She was, however, a Union spy, who acquired maps and sketches of military importance at Chickamauga and Chattanooga. Braxton Bragg's men eventually found her out, she was arrested, and subsequently sentenced to hang. Fortunately for Pauline, Federal troops rescued her before sentence could be carried out.

Early in the war, the punishment for espionage tended to be lenient; Rose Greenhow, spying for the South in 1861, was arrested, confined briefly, and then "paroled" to the Confederacy. But, after two years of bloodletting on the battlefield, both sides found that executing a spy was no longer unthinkable, even if the accused was a woman—or a seventeen-year-old boy. David O. Dodd was a Confederate courier arrested by Federal troops near Little Rock, Arkansas:

Military Prison, Little Rock
January 8, 10 o'clock a.m., 1864

My Dear Parents and Sisters:

 I was arrested as a spy and tried and was sentenced to be hung today at 3 o'clock. The time is fast approaching, but, thank God! I am prepared to die. I expect to meet you all in Heaven. I will soon be out of this world of sorrow and trouble. I would like to see you all before I die, but let God's will be done, not ours. I pray to God to give you strength to bear your troubles while in this world. I hope God will receive you in Heaven; there I will meet you.

 Mother, I know it will be hard for you to give up your only son, but you must remember it is God's will. Goodbye! God will give you strength to bear your troubles. I pray that we may meet in Heaven. Goodbye! God will bless you all.

Your son and brother,
David O. Dodd

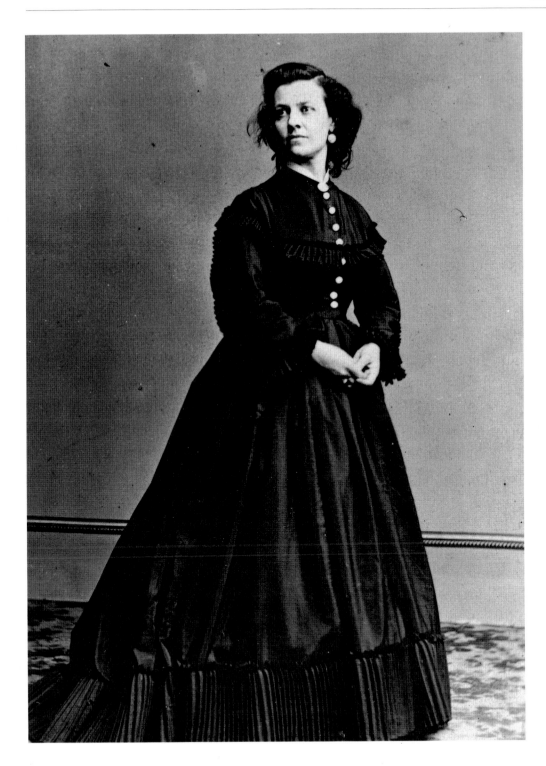

Corporal Charles E. Brown survived the war unscathed, serving in the 122nd Illinois until July 1865, when he transferred to Company E, 33rd Illinois Volunteers. His reenlistment earned him the "veteran stripe" chevron below his corporal's stripes. Arthur van Lisle was not so lucky:

I fall. I try to rise, but cannot. . . . My thigh is torn, the bone is shattered, although I did not feel the shot that struck me. Here I lie among the dead and wounded. Our men have fallen back. Over our prostrate forms the bullets are hissing and shells shrieking. In the endeavor to ease my cramped position my wounded limb becomes twisted; and, oh, the agony of pain which I now feel for the first time! What horror surrounds me! Here I am, helpless and bleeding, my flesh lacerated, my thigh-bone broken; the dead so ghastly, the dying and the wounded all about me; my regiment falling back, the enemy advancing. What will become of me?

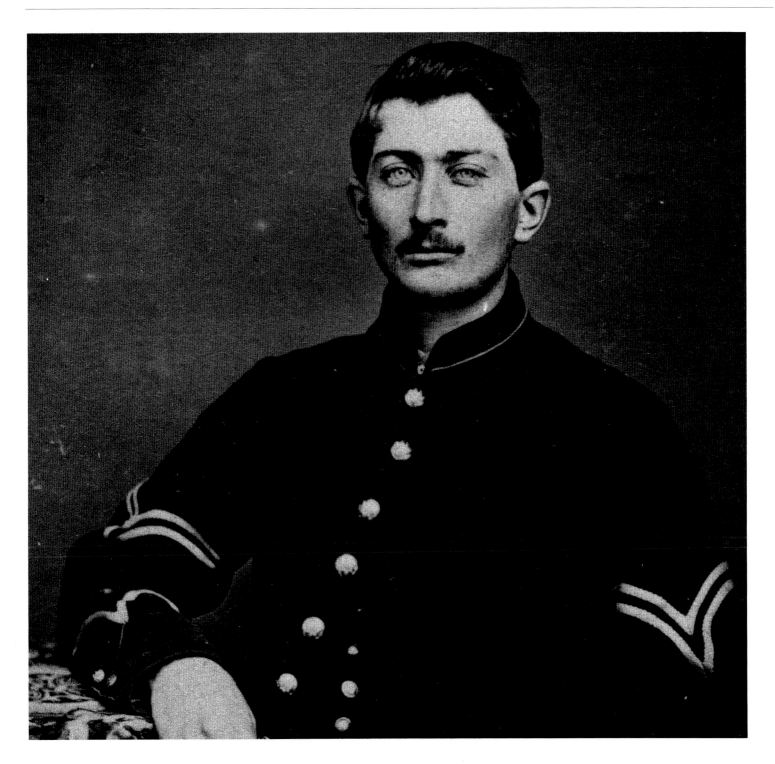

THE WILDERNESS, SPOTSYLVANIA, AND COLD HARBOR

May 5–7, May 7–20, May 31–June 12, 1864

When Abraham Lincoln made Ulysses S. Grant commanding general in 1864, Grant prepared a strategy for all Union forces: four coordinated, simultaneous blows against the Confederate armies in the field. Benjamin Butler would lead an army up the James River; Franz Sigel would work his way along the Shenandoah Valley; William Tecumseh Sherman would strike out from Chattanooga for Atlanta; and George Meade, directly under Grant, would chase Lee and *fight* him, wherever he went.

Lee, for his part, planned to make Grant pay dearly for every engagement until he destroyed the North's will to wage war. If he could fight Grant to a bloody draw, chances were Lincoln would lose the upcoming election, and the United States would sue for peace.

The photograph shows the Union's Army of the Potomac crossing Germanna Ford on the Rapidan River (an artillery battery moves across the nearer pontoon bridge), advancing toward the Wilderness, where Lee had trapped the hapless "Fighting Joe" Hooker the year before. Grant's advance units camped on May 4, 1864, on the old Chancellorsville battlefield among shallow graves washed open by winter rains.

The fighting began at noon the next day, and chaos reigned. Units wandered about lost, firing on their own comrades, as benighted officers tried to maneuver by compass on a battlefield with no lines. It was the first day of the six bloodiest weeks of the war, fought without break as Grant tried over and over to get around Lee's right flank, move on to Richmond, and end the war.

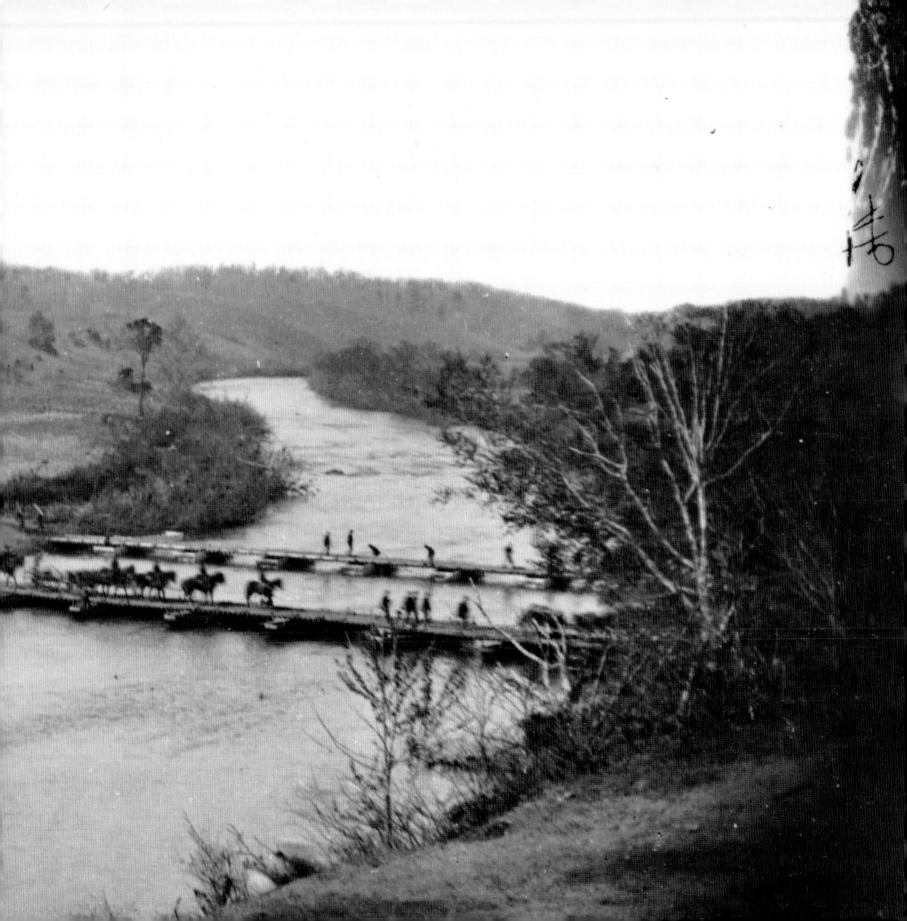

Grant lost 17,000 men during the first two days of the Wilderness campaign. But instead of retreating, he ordered his men south. Lee guessed correctly that he was headed for Spotsylvania and was waiting when Grant arrived on May 11. At dawn, Grant sent 20,000 men against the Confederate center and captured the Confederate breastworks along a curved salient called the Mule Shoe. Lee counterattacked and reclaimed the log works, but the battle continued, surging back and forth all day. The two armies lost 12,000 men, and Lee fell back, as the fighting continued here and there around Spotsylvania for several days.

Then the armies began to move again. Lee would seek to elude Grant for a while, then attack. Grant would try to skirt south and east to get around him, then stop and fight. For almost a month, the dogged Grant chased Robert E. Lee through the wilderness down the length of Virginia. Then the two armies began a race for the crossroads called Cold Harbor, just off the Chickahominy River southeast of Richmond.

Lee got there first and entrenched his troops for the all-out assault he knew the gruesomely determined Grant would throw at him. Grant's buglers blew the charge at 4:30 A.M. on June 3, and 60,000 bluecoats moved on an invisible enemy. The Confederate guns roared, and whole Union regiments disappeared in geysers of dirt and erupting sand.

When it was over, not a Yankee was left standing. Counting casualties was almost impossible, but around 7,000 Union soldiers fell at Cold Harbor, the majority of them in the first eight minutes. Northern commanders simply refused to send any more of their soldiers to the slaughter, and for three days and three nights the two armies just sat there, neither commander willing to ask for a truce to collect the wounded or bury the dead.

Nearly five acres were piled thick with the dead and the dying. A lucky few crawled to safety. At least one wounded soldier, unable to do so, slit his throat in plain sight of his fellow combatants. By the time litter bearers were finally let onto the battleground, *two* of the thousands of Union wounded were still alive. Grant himself later admitted that he regretted as much as anything he had ever done giving the order to attack at Cold Harbor.

———

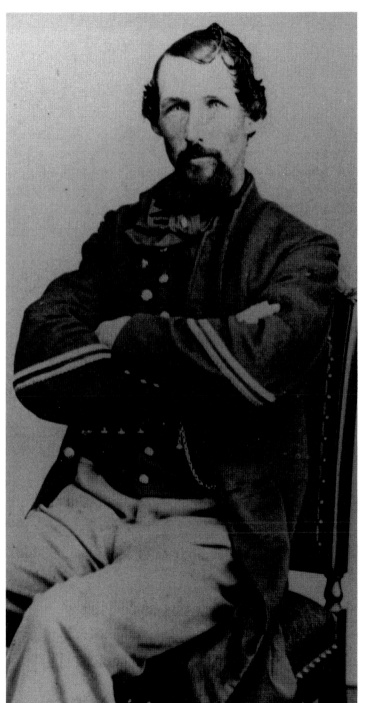

A. M. Stewart, chaplain to a Pennsylvania regiment, reported on the Spotsylvania fight in letters published at the end of the war in his *Camp, March and Battle-field*:

As to how we came here [Hanover Court House] from Spotsylvania Court House, a volume would scarcely suffice to tell. What skirmishings and fightings—what long, long, weary marches by day and night—what countermarches, now far to the right, again away to the left—passing over hot, dusty roads, corduroy bridges, and pontoons; through mud, creeks, fields, woods, swamps, and sloughs; amid moonlight and thick darkness, showers, thunderstorms, and sunshine.

Much of this may never, can never be written; and were it, could not be understood by those not exercised therein.

Among the fighters and the marchers was Private Charles F. Belcher, pictured here, of Company K, 1st Massachusetts Heavy Artillery. His unit was pulled from duty defending Washington on May 15, 1864 and saw action at Spotsylvania on May 19. Assigned to II Corps, Army of the Potomac, Belcher's regiment also fought at Cold Harbor and Petersburg. In the latter fight, on June 16, Belcher received what his service record calls a "slight wound." It resulted in the amputation of the ring finger and little finger of his left hand.

In context, perhaps it was indeed a "slight" wound. From the time the 1st Massachusetts Heavy Artillery left Washington in mid-May through the end of June, the regiment lost forty-six officers and 890 enlisted men, killed, wounded, captured, or missing. Heavy artillery regiments had twelve companies (infantry regiments generally had ten); estimating that the average heavy artillery company mustered 110 men, it is likely that this unit took about 1,300 officers and men into the field. This means that, in the space of six weeks, the 1st Massachusetts suffered a 72 percent casualty rate.

Trenches and rifle pits were not the invention of the twentieth century's two world wars. The photograph shows Confederate entrenchments on the Spotsylvania battlefield. The Union dug in, too. Caught in a storm of lead and steel splinters, troops learned to hug the ground, but conditions in rifle pits and trenches soon became all but intolerable, as Chaplain Stewart recalled:

From where I stood, and in front of a Rebel rifle pit, lay stretched in all positions over fifty of our unburied soldiers, and within the pit and lying across each other, perhaps as many Rebel dead. It seems almost incredible what a change of little less than a week had wrought, by exposure to sun and hot air. The hair and skin had fallen from the head, and the flesh from the bones—all alive with disgusting maggots.

Many of the soldiers stuffed their nostrils with green leaves. Such a scene does seem too revolting to record. Yet, how else convey any just conception of what is done and suffered here?

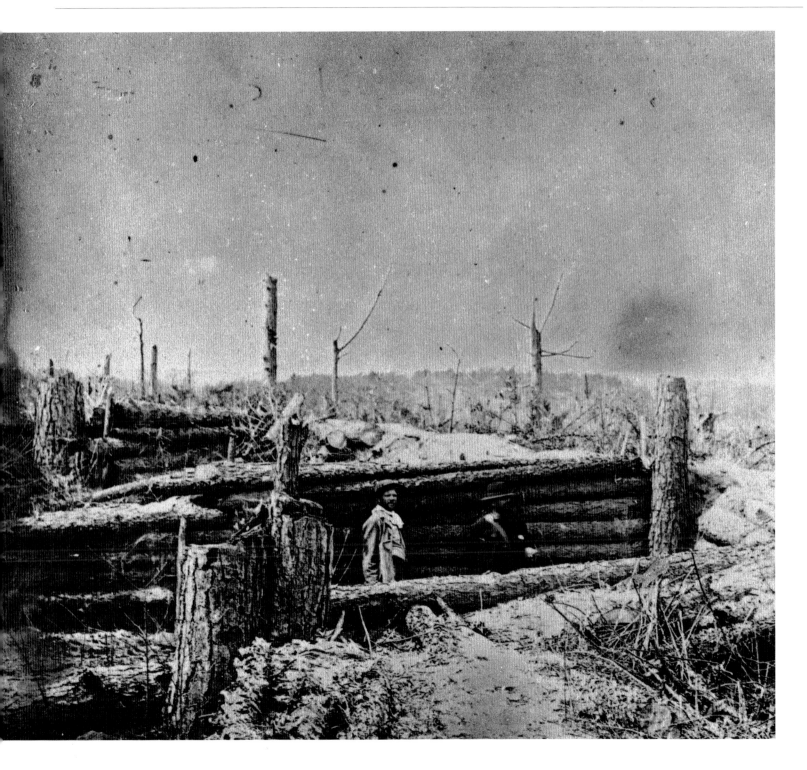

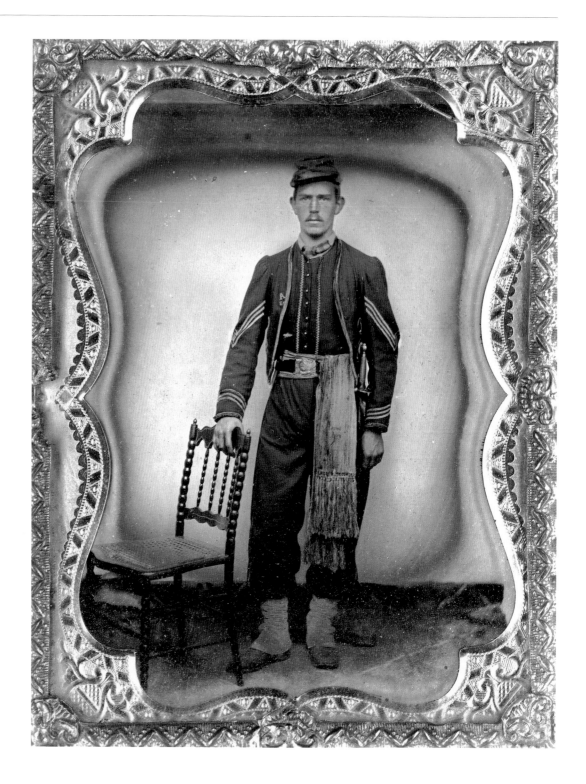

Daniel Chisholm, Company K, 116th Pennsylvania Regiment, wrote home from Cold Harbor on June 8, 1864:

Tell mother not to be uneasy about us after battles for if not killed or wounded we will always write as soon as possible.

Pictured here is an unidentified sergeant of the 23rd Massachusetts Volunteers. As part of XVII Corps, the unit fought at Cold Harbor on June 3.

Daniel Chisholm kept a diary:

Tuesday, June 7th - Cold Harbor

At 2 O'clock this morning they made a long determined charge, but the boys never wavered. We could hear the Reb officers shouting forward, forward. On they came but it was only to be mowed down by the Thousand. We never thought of getting drove out, I rather enjoyed it and I believe the rest of the boys did also. At daylight this morning all was quiet. The enemy advanced a white Flag, asking permission to bury their dead, which was granted. We had an armistice of two hours. The quietness was really oppressive, It positively made us feel lonesome, after a continual racket day and night for so long. We sit on the works and let our legs dangle over on the front and watch the Johnnies carry off their dead comrades in silence, but in a great hurry. Some of them lay dead within twenty feet of our works — the live Rebel looks bad enough in his old torn, ragged Butternut suit, but a dead Rebel looks horrible all swelled up and black in the face. After they were through there was nothing left but stains of Blood, broken and twisted guns, old hats, canteens, every one of them reminders of the death and carnage that reigned a few short hours before. When the 2 hours was up we got back in our holes and they did the same. A large gun at the fort gave one shot and both sides passed a few but no damage was done. Things quieted down except the continual crack of the Sharpshooters rifles. They are busy from daylight until dark, they hide in trees, behind stumps, along banks, or where ever they can protect themselves and see their enemies.

Sergeant Joseph E. Averill, Company K, 6th Vermont Infantry, which fought at Cold Harbor, is pictured here. ✎

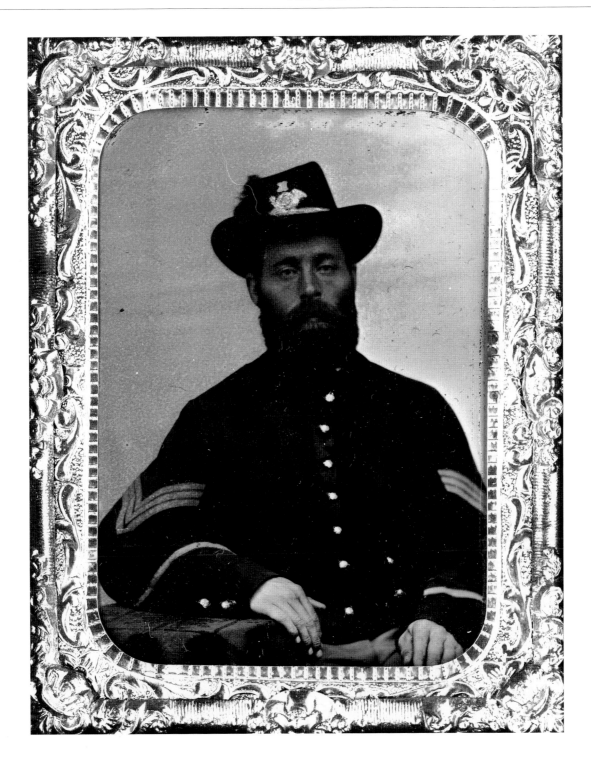

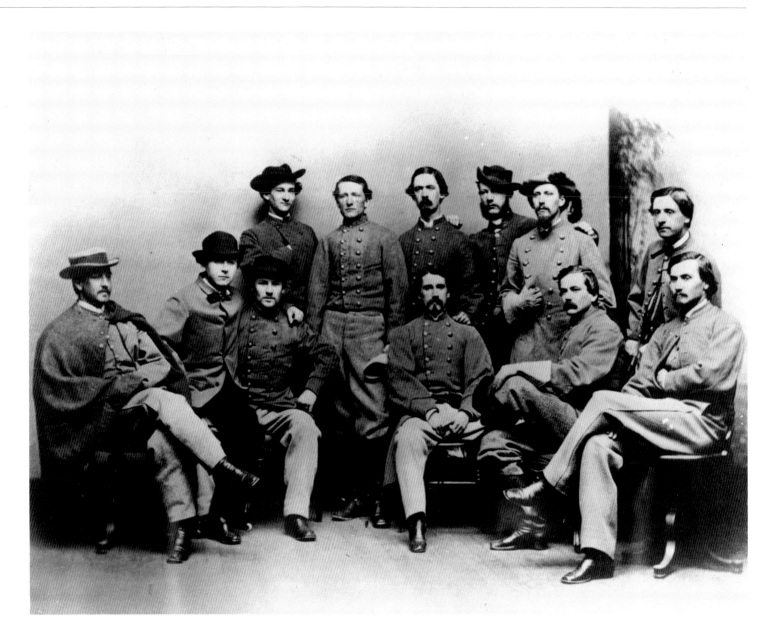

Amid the horrors of battles like the Wilderness, Spotsylvania, and Cold Harbor, Lieutenant Colonel John Singleton Mosby (standing second from left) and his "Partisan Rangers" (mustered into the regular Confederate army on June 10, 1863 as the 43rd Virginia Cavalry Battalion) kept alive a spark of romance with their daring and immediately legendary guerrilla exploits. Not only did Mosby's raids accomplish significant military ends (one historian believes that, by diverting Grant's strength, his actions significantly prolonged the life of the Confederacy), the "Gray Ghost" had a certain *style*. In March of 1863, he captured Brigadier General Edwin H. Stoughton, taking him from his bed and ceremoniously slapping him on the behind. *That* is a wound from which there can be no recovery.

Panache alone is not enough to win a war, of course, and by the time of the Wilderness Campaign, as Confederate artilleryman Robert Stiles reluctantly observed, the spirit of the beleaguered Southern army was showing signs of strain. Stiles talked to a friend who had just returned from furlough and had spent the night with an infantry regiment that "contained many of his former schoolmates and friends and neighbors":

He did not detect any depression or apprehension of disaster or weakness of pluck or purpose; but he says he did miss the bounding, buoyant spirit . . .

. . . if one army outnumbers another more than two to one, and the larger can be indefinitely reinforced and the smaller not at all, then if the stronger side will but make up its mind to stand all the killing the weaker can do, and will keep it so made up, there can be but one result.

Billy says the realization of this new order of things did not affect the resolution of the men, but that it did affect their spirits. I can only say I believe he is exactly correct.

Mary Edwards Walker, born in Oswego, New York, on November 26, 1832, bucked the male-dominated medical establishment by winning admission to and graduation from Syracuse Medical College. During the 1840s and 1850s, she struggled to survive in her Cincinnati, Ohio practice, gaining little acceptance as a physician from either sex. With the outbreak of the war, Walker volunteered her medical services in the only capacity the Union army would allow: as a nurse. Early in 1864, an Ohio regiment hired her as a "contract surgeon" for six months, and, in October of that year, the Union army at last commissioned her as an assistant surgeon.

During her tour of duty, she saw service not only as a physician, but as a spy. Walker, who was known for looking after wounded on both sides, was captured by Confederates when she had stopped to treat a wounded Rebel. She spent four months in a Southern prison camp.

Walker was the first woman to be awarded the Congressional Medal of Honor. In 1919, however, the Board of Medals revoked the award. "You can have it over my dead body," the eighty-seven-year-old physician told the Federal authorities who gave her the news of the revocation. Six days later she died. (The medal was officially and posthumously restored to her in 1977.)

Walt Whitman, who volunteered as a civilian nurse at periods during the war, was keenly aware of the difficulties the Union's surgeons faced—first because there were so few doctors and so many wounded, and, second, because there never were enough medical supplies:

Of all harrowing experiences, none is greater than that of the days following a heavy battle. Scores, hundreds of the noblest men on earth, uncomplaining, lie helpless, mangled, faint, alone, and so bleed to death, or die from exhaustion, either totally untouch'd at all, or merely the laying of them down and leaving them, when there ought to be means provided to save them.

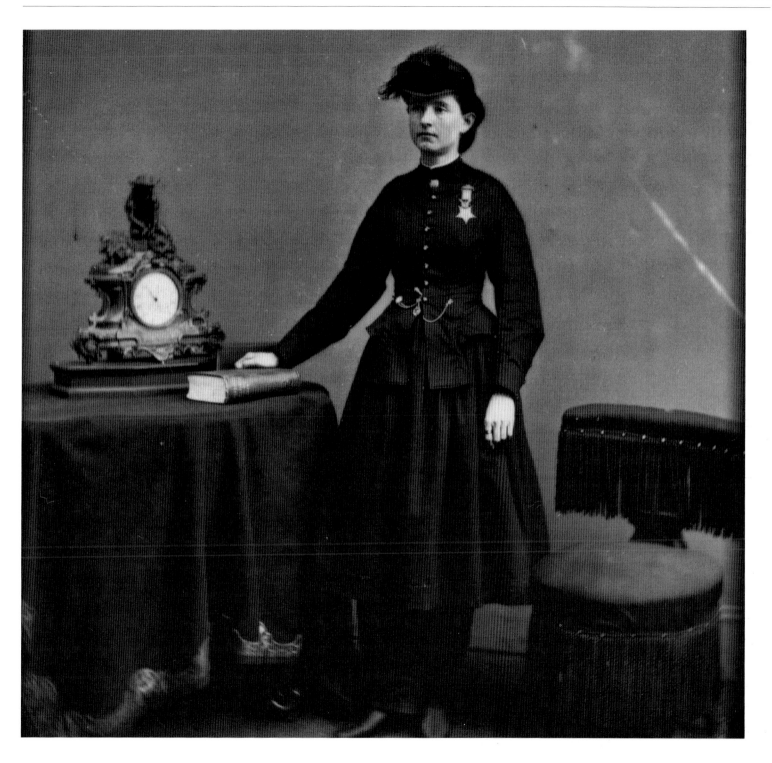

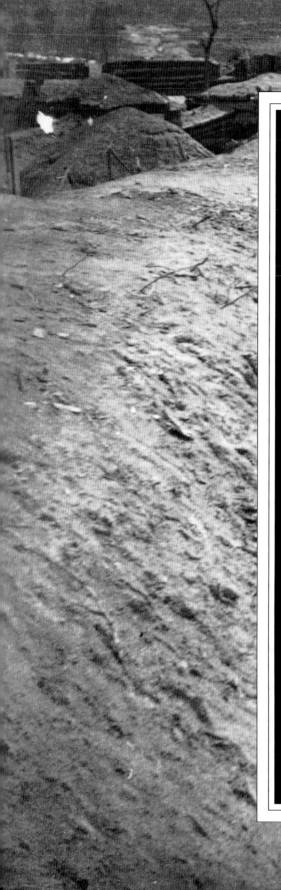
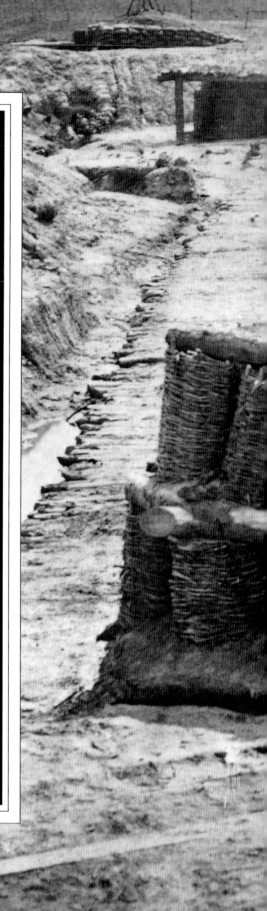

PETERSBURG

June 1864–May 1865

The fighting in the Wilderness ended when Ulysses S. Grant slipped his army out of its trenches under the cover of darkness and crossed the Chickahominy, evidently heading toward Richmond. At least Robert E. Lee thought so, and he rushed the majority of his troops to the outskirts of the city. Grant, however, shifted left to the James River and his real target, Petersburg, a communications center just south of the Confederate capital. If he took Petersburg, Grant reasoned, he could choke off Richmond just as he had Vicksburg the year before.

For once Lee was surprised, and when the first 16,000 Federal troops arrived at Petersburg on June 15, 1864, only 3,000 Rebels under Beauregard were on hand to defend it. The Union soldiers, commanded by General W. F. "Baldy" Smith, were combat weary, with the slaughter at Cold Harbor fresh in their memories, and they were slow to attack. When expected reinforcements got lost on the way and failed to arrive, Smith called off the fight with victory virtually in hand. Beauregard was reinforced, and the war went on as repeated assaults were beaten back, and both sides settled in for a siege.

Six weeks of constant combat had crippled both armies; now they burrowed into the ground, creating a labyrinth of trenches exposed to rain and mortar fire and plagued by fires and disease. For ten months the two sides faced each other across a landscape that half a century later would become the very image of modern warfare when it was reproduced by the belligerants of

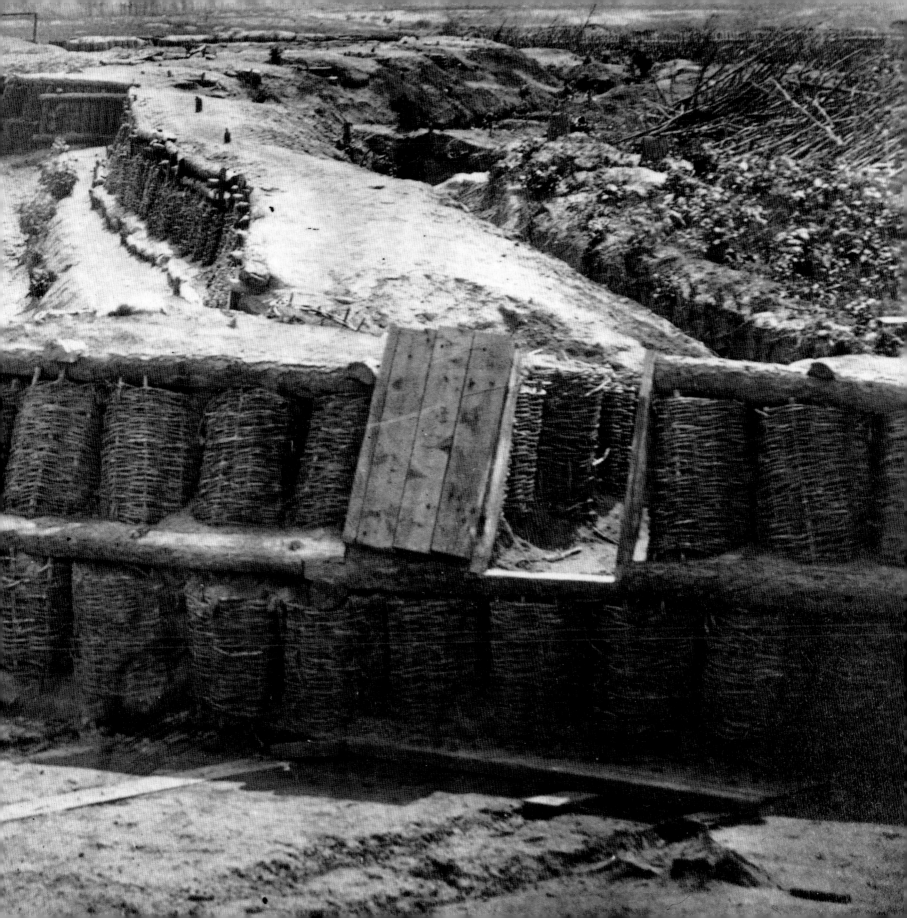

World War I. The photograph is of the Union's siege lines, which were christened Fort Sedgwick.

Early in the campaign, toward the end of July, a regiment of Pennsylvania coal miners persuaded General Burnside to let them try a desperate gamble. They would build a tunnel underneath the Confederate lines and blow a hole in them wide enough to march an army through. The first half of the plan worked remarkably well. The miners built their tunnel, loaded it with explosives, and blew a huge crater in the Rebel defenses that sent Southerners reeling back in terror. But an hour went by before the follow-up assault got started, and when it did, three divisions rushed into the hole instead of around it. They had forgotten even to bring ladders, and as they milled about in the thirty-foot pit it occurred to both sides they were trapped.

The Rebels regrouped and commenced firing, and by afternoon the Union troops surrendered. The Confederates took white troops captive, but they shot, bayonetted, and bludgeoned to death hundreds of black soldiers who approached them under a white flag.

As the siege continued, Union troops fought their way west, cutting off the last road into the town from the south and threatening the last open railroad. Lee's army had by then begun to desert in large numbers, and as spring dried up the muddy roads after an exceptionally raw and wet winter, Lee realized it was only a matter of time; he knew he soon would have to abandon Petersburg—and with it, Richmond—if he wanted to keep his army from being encircled.

On May 24, 1865, he launched a surprise attack on Grant east of Petersburg in a desperate bid to force the Union commander to contract the Union lines blocking a Rebel escape. Instead, Grant counterattacked and captured many of the Rebels, and Lee's own lines grew so thin that they could not hold. With the arrival of Sheridan's cavalry from the Shenandoah Valley, Grant attacked the Confederate right on March 29, a move that two days later resulted in the most one-sided Union victory since the beginning of the Wilderness campaign eleven months earlier. When Grant heard that George Pickett's two divisions had collapsed in surrender and rout, he ordered an assault all along the line for the next morning.

It came at dawn on April 2. The Army of Northern Virginia fought desperately as the Yankees punched through Confederate lines, trying to hold its inner defenses just until dark in order to escape. Lee sent a message to President Jefferson Davis to flee Richmond, and the next day Abraham Lincoln himself followed his troops into the erstwhile Rebel capital.

———

Esther Hill Hawks, a physician, teacher, suffragist, and abolitionist, went to Georgia's Sea Islands in 1864 to minister to African American Union troops both as a teacher and a doctor. Among those she treated were 150 soldiers of the 54th Massachusetts, wounded in the suicidally gallant assault on Fort Wagner. Hawks recorded in her diary:

It was a busy time, and the amount of work done in that 24 hours, by the two surgeons, and one sick woman [Hawks herself] is tiresome to remember! The only thing that sustained us was the patient endurance of those stricken heroes lying before us, with their wounds cheerful & courageous, many a poor fellow sighing that his right arm was shattered beyond hope of striking another blow for freedom! Only a few weeks before we had welcomed them as they marched so proudly through our streets with their idolized leader Col. Shaw, at their head!—How all the colored people cheered and gloried in their fine appearance—and now the people are so eager to show their pride in them that they constantly deny themselves in order to bring gifts to the hospital!

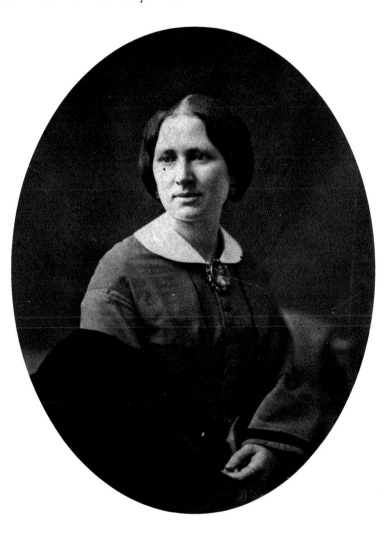

Officers attached to U.S. Major General Orlando B. Wilcox's IX Corps headquarters, Petersburg lines, enjoy a smoke and a cockfight. The black men handling the birds are "contrabands"—runaway slaves who often worked as servants in and around Federal camps. General Sherman's aide-de-camp, Major George Ward Nichols, published his diary after the war, in which he noted, among much else, the popularity in camp of "the hero of the barnyard":

There is not a regiment nor a company, not a teamster nor a Negro at headquarters, nor an orderly, but has a rooster of one kind or another. When the column is moving, these haughty gamecocks are seen mounted upon the breech of a cannon, tied to the pack-saddle of a mule among pots and pans, or carried lovingly in the arms of a mounted orderly; crowing with all his might from the interior of a wagon, or making the woods re-echo with his triumphant notes as he rides perched upon the knapsack of a soldier.

These cocks represent every known breed, Polish and Spanish, Dorkings, Shanghais and Bantams—high-blooded specimens traveling with [others] of their species who may not boast of noble lineage. They must all fight, however, or be killed and eaten.

Hardly has the army gone into camp before these feathery combats begin. The cocks use only the spurs with which Nature furnishes them . . . and so but little harm is done. The gamecocks which have come out of repeated conflicts victorious are honored with such names as "Bill Sherman," "Johnny Logan," etc., while the defeated and bepecked victim is saluted with derisive appellations such as "Jeff Davis," "Beauregard," or "Bob Lee."

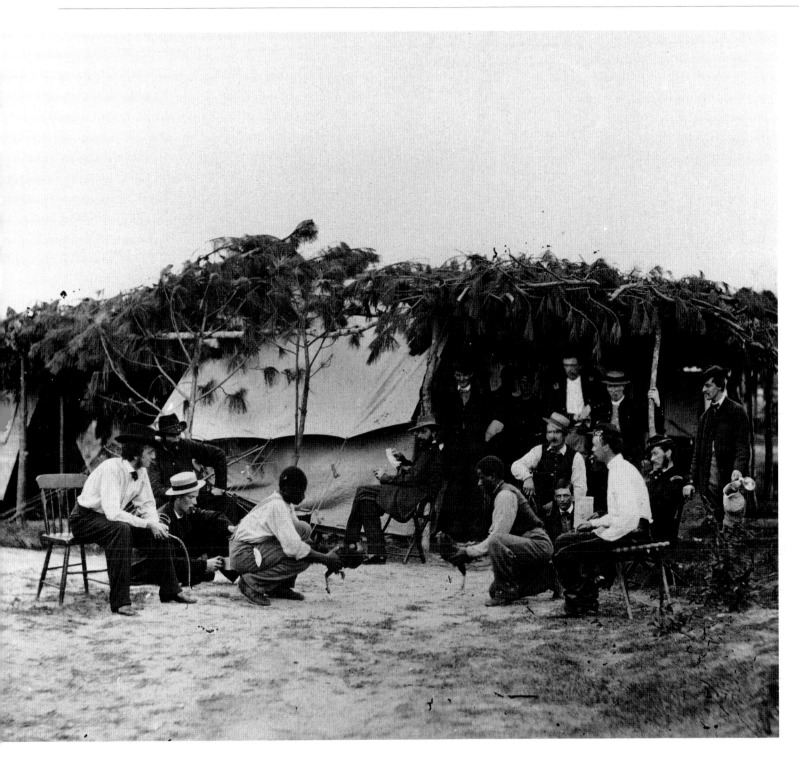

These soldiers are members of Company E, 4th U.S. Colored Troops, a unit formed in Baltimore late in the summer of 1863. Taking into consideration that African American units were characteristically treated with contempt by Army quartermasters, these men are decently equipped. Except for the first sergeant and the man to his left, who wear shell jackets, the troops are outfitted in frock coats. Most of them even sport full-dress shoulder scales. Not all of the men have cartridge-belt slings, and, among those who do, the breast plate is often missing. The unit saw hard fighting at New Market Heights in September 1864 and participated in attacks against the massive Rebel bastion, Fort Fisher, North Carolina.

One Jerry Sullivan spoke out at a black rally in Union-held Nashville, Tennessee:

God is in this war. He will lead us on to victory. Folks talk about the fighting being nearly over, but I believe there is a heap yet to come. Let the colored men accept the offer of the President and Cabinet, take arms, join the army, and then we will whip the rebels, even if Longstreet and all the Streets of the South, concentrate at Chattanooga. (Laughter and applause.) Why, don't you remember how afraid they used to be that we would rise? And you know we would, too, if we could. (Cries of "that's so.") I ran away two years ago. . . . I got to Cincinnati, and from there I went straight to General Rosecrans' headquarters. And now I am going to be Corporal. (Shouts of laughter.)

Come, boys, let's get some guns from Uncle Sam, and go coon hunting; shooting those grey back coons that go poking about the country now a days. (Laughter.) Tomorrow morning, don't eat too much breakfast, but as soon as you get back from market, start the first thing for our camp. Don't ask your wife, for if she is a wife worth having she will call you a coward for asking her. (Applause, and waving of handkerchiefs by the ladies.) I've got a wife and she says to me, the other day, "Jerry, if you don't go to the war mighty soon, I'll go off and leave you, as some of the Northern gentlemen want me to go home to cook for them." (Laughter.) . . . The ladies are now busy making us a flag, and let us prove ourselves men worthy to bear it.

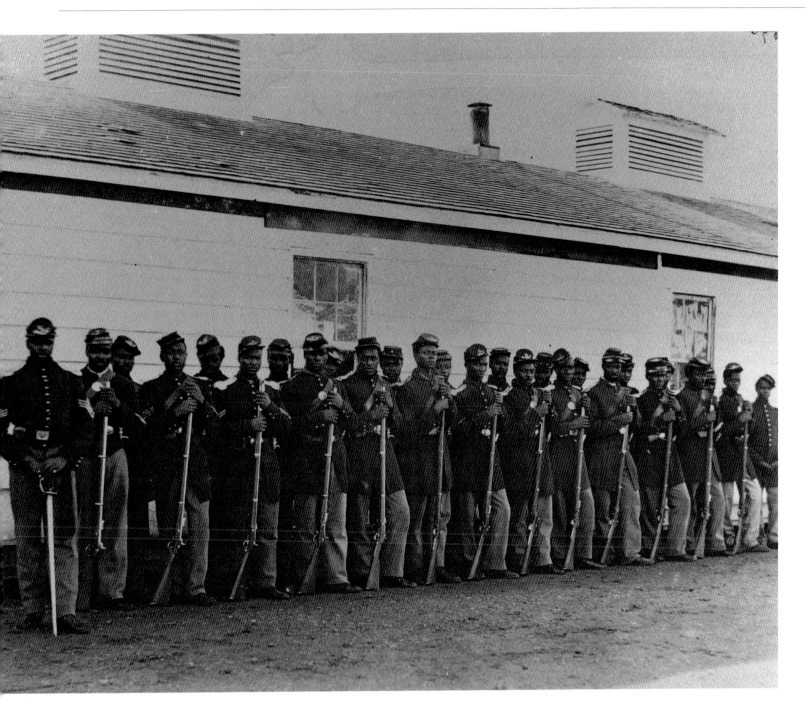

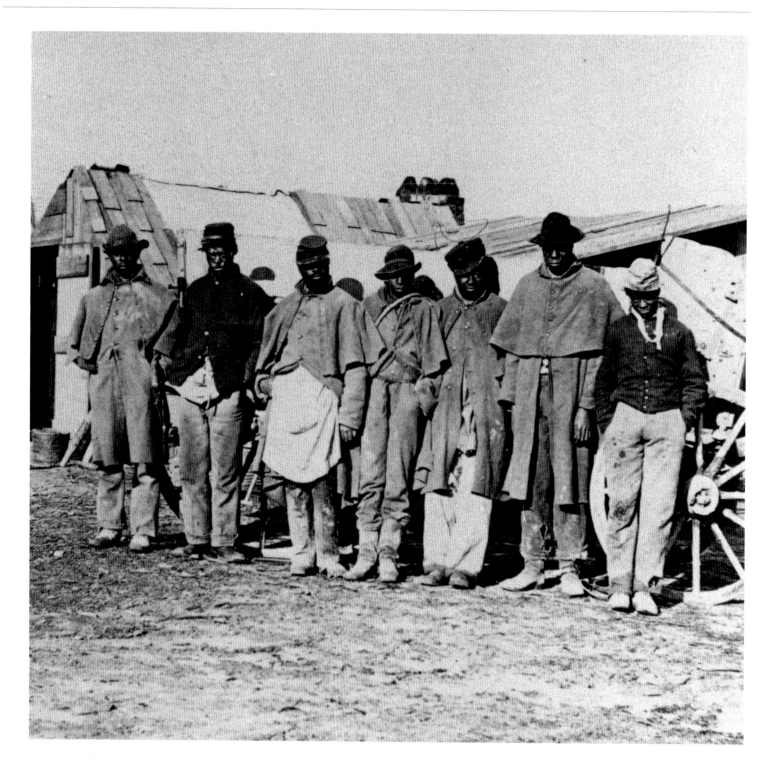

Clothed in cast-off uniforms, these U.S. Army teamsters were part of a vast logistical force that kept Grant supplied around Petersburg and Richmond. Many African Americans, runaway slaves, former slaves, and free men, were eager to serve in the Union Army, which, as they saw it, was fighting for their collective liberation. Although in August 1862, Union General Ben Butler raised the Louisiana Native Guards (also known as the Corps d'Afrique) and, a month later, an unarmed and uniformless black brigade was organized in Cincinnati to combat Morgan's raiders, the recruitment of African American troops met with bitter resistance. Abraham Lincoln had personally vetoed a second and a third Louisiana brigade and put an end to recruitment of African Americans in occupied South Carolina. However, Rhode Island, Kansas, and Massachusetts soon called for black enlistment, and, with the signing of the Emancipation Proclamation on January 1, 1863, Lincoln himself had called for four African American regiments.

By the end of the war, approximately 300,000 African Americans were under arms in segregated regiments commanded by white officers. Given the opportunity to fight, African American troops usually distinguished themselves. The single most celebrated unit was the 54th Massachusetts, which lost 272 men (including their commander, Colonel Robert Gould Shaw) of the 650 engaged in an assault on Fort Wagner, South Carolina, on July 18, 1863. Most often, however, black troops were relegated to manual labor and teamster assignments.

Frederick Douglass's plea in August 1861 was among the first and most eloquent of many:

The national edifice is on fire. Every man who can carry a bucket of water, or remove a brick, is wanted; but those who have the care of the building, having a profound respect for the feeling of the national burglars who set the building on fire, are determined that the flames shall only be extinguished by Indo-Caucasian hands, and to have the building burnt rather than save it by means of any other. Such is the pride, the stupid prejudice and folly that rules the hour.

Why does the Government reject the negro? Is he not a man? Can he not wield a sword, fire a gun, march and countermarch, and obey orders like any other? . . . If persons so humble as we can be allowed to speak to the President of the United States, we should ask him if this dark and terrible hour of the nation's extremity is a time for consulting a mere vulgar and unnatural prejudice? . . . We would tell him that this is no time to fight with one hand, when both are needed; that this is no time to fight only with your white hand, and allow your black hand to remain tied. . . . Men in earnest don't fight with one hand, when they might fight with two, and a man drowning would not refuse to be saved even by a colored hand.

Garrett Nowlin (also spelled Nolan and Nolen) was a second lieutenant, Company G, when the 116th Pennsylvania Volunteers—part of the celebrated Irish Brigade—mustered in during August 1862. In January 1863, the men of the 116th were consolidated into four companies, and Nowlin, severely wounded in the thigh at Fredericksburg, transferred in grade to what had become Company D. On March 1, 1863, he was made regimental adjutant and was promoted to captain on November 21. During 1864, still holding the rank of captain, he took command of the regiment. Soldier-diarist Daniel Chisholm was at the Battle of Ream's Station, during the siege of Petersburg, when Nowlin was killed on August 25, 1864:

We advanced over in a murderous fire. Just as we reached the skirmish line the rebels with two lines of battle emerged from the woods. We was then ordered back to the works, but we had lost twenty one killed and wounded in that half hour. Capt Nolen of Co B [sic] commanded the Regt, he went along the line and encouraged us to stand firm, and not to fire until he gave the word. As he spoke the last word a bullet from a sharpshooters rifle pierced his breast and he fell, his last and only words were tell Capt Taggart Co I to take command. Capt Taggart was going along the lines repeating the same orders given by Capt Nolen when he was shot through the heart, he never spoke again. There fell two of as brave Captain as ever drew swords.

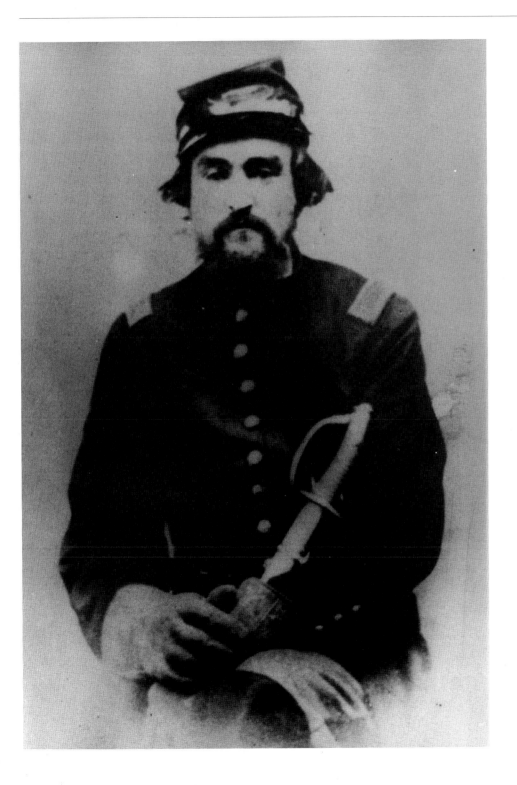

THE FALL OF ATLANTA
AND THE MARCH TO THE SEA

September 2, 1864
November 14–December 22, 1864

Starting from Chattanooga on May 6, 1864, William Tecumseh Sherman rolled inexorably south, chasing the Rebel forces under Joseph T. Johnston out of one position after another, right up to the heavily fortified city of Atlanta. The photograph shows the city's defensive works and some of the houses cannibalized for wood to erect them.

Sherman was stalled before the city for the rest of the summer of 1864. When Johnston hinted that he might abandon Atlanta if need be, Davis replaced him in mid-June with the more aggressive John Bell Hood. Throughout the first half of August, Sherman's cavalry and Hood's raided each other but to little effect, while the Union infantry futilely probed south toward the railroad below Atlanta. When most of Sherman's army disappeared suddenly on August 26, Hood concluded rashly that Sherman had retreated. Instead, Sherman had taken his troops far south of the Confederate defenses to cut all roads and railroads leading into the city. By the time Hood realized what had happened, it was too late. To avoid being trapped, he gave up Atlanta. The city's inhabitants packed up what they could and fled. The next day, bands blaring and flags waving, the bluecoats marched in.

Hood continued to harass Sherman's rear areas, trying to cut his supply lines from Chattanooga. But Sherman had had enough of that kind of fighting. He told Grant: "I could cut a swath to the sea, divide the Confederacy in two, and come up on the rear of Lee." Sherman had in mind what would later be called total war. He would march his whole army to Savannah, cutting loose from his base of supply, living off the land, and destroying everything in his path that could aid the enemy. His object was nothing less than to crush the will of the Southern people, and as Sherman left Atlanta, he ordered a third of it burned. In the wake of his departure, poor whites and blacks plundered what was left.

Sherman's 62,000 men traveled in two huge columns, trailing a supply train that stretched twenty-five miles. Along the way, they picked up fellow travelers—freed slaves, scoundrels, and freebooters called "bummers"—many along for the plunder in what one of his soldiers described as "the greatest pleasure trip ever planned." Nothing stopped him. In addition to tearing up railroads and raiding farms, his men hacked down whole forests to build corduroy roads. In South Carolina, his treatment of the citizenry was even harsher than in Georgia, for he felt that there was the region where the Confederate treason had begun. Sherman was transformed by his march into one of the most hated men in Southern history, and the march itself became the symbol—much more than Lee's surrender to Grant—of the South's defeat and humiliation.

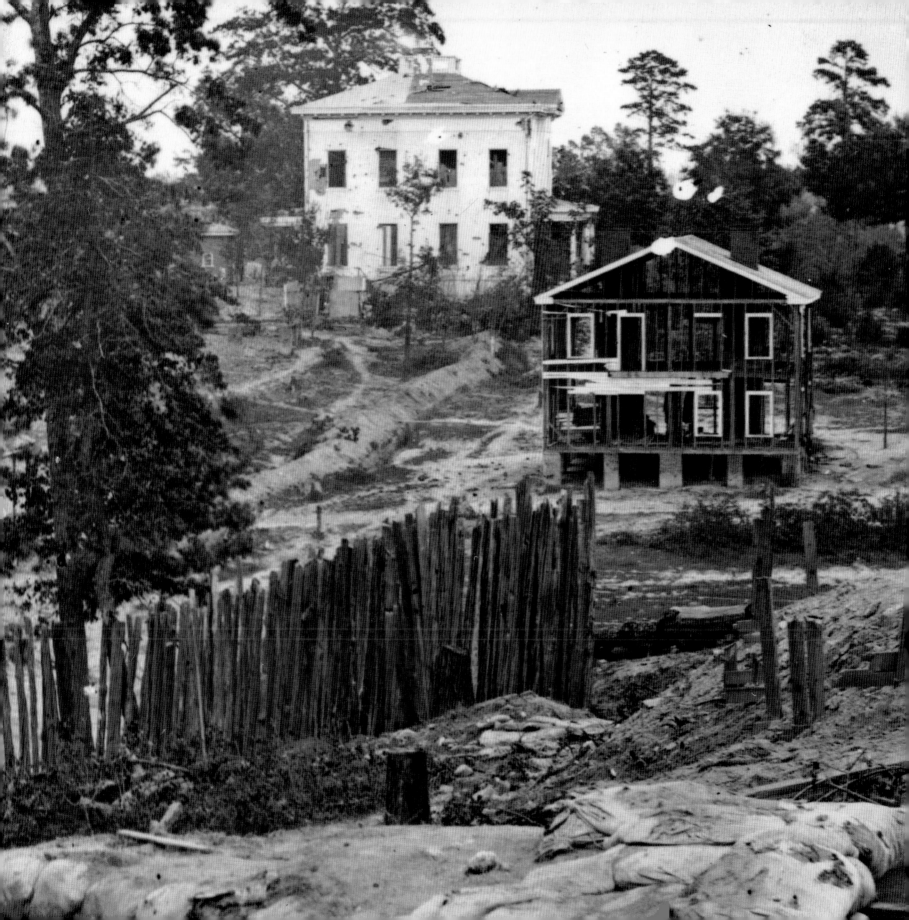

Even before his death in 1891, William Tecumseh Sherman had become associated with the phrase "War is hell." However, this advocate of the doctrine of "total warfare" (war waged not only against military objectives but against enemy civilians as well) could not recall ever having said quite that. But he had responded in this vein to the appeal of Atlanta's mayor and city councilmen, who protested his order to evacuate Atlanta. Asserting the military necessity of the evacuation, Sherman wrote:

You cannot qualify war in harsher terms than I will. War is cruelty, and you cannot refine it. And those who brought war into our country deserve all the curses and maledictions a people can pour out. . . .

You might as well appeal against the thunderstorm as against the terrible hardships of war. They are inevitable, and the only way the people of Atlanta can hope once more to live in peace and quiet at home is to stop the war. . . .

. . . I want peace, and I believe it can only be reached through Union and war; and I will ever conduct war purely with a view to perfect an early success. But, my dear sirs, when peace does come, you may call on me for anything. Then will I share with you the last cracker, and watch with you to shield your homes and families against danger from every quarter.

Now you must go, and take with you the old and feeble, feed and nurse them, and build for them in more quiet places proper habitations to shield them against the weather until the mad passions of men cool down and allow the Union and peace once more to settle over your old homes at Atlanta.

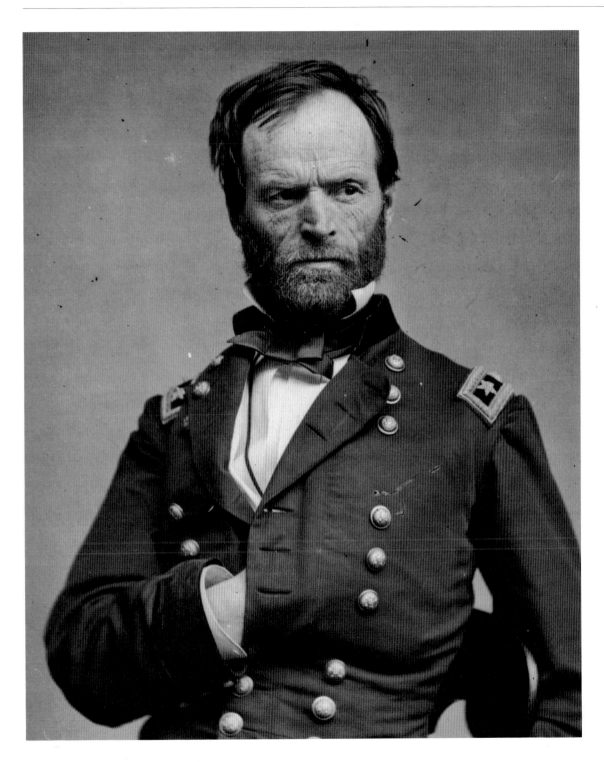

Sherman's aide-de-camp, Major George Ward Nichols, recorded in his diary, which was published immediately after the war:

A grand and awful spectacle is presented to the beholder in this beautiful city, now in flames. By order, the chief engineer has destroyed by powder and fire all the store-houses, depot buildings, and machine-shops. The heaven is one expanse of lurid fire; the air is filled with flying, burning cinders; buildings covering two hundred acres are in ruins or flames; every instant there is a sharp detonation or the smothered booming sound of exploding shells and powder concealed in the buildings, and then the sparks and flame shoot away up into the black and red roofs, scattering cinders far and wide.

The photograph is of an enlisted man in a unit of Federal horse artillery.

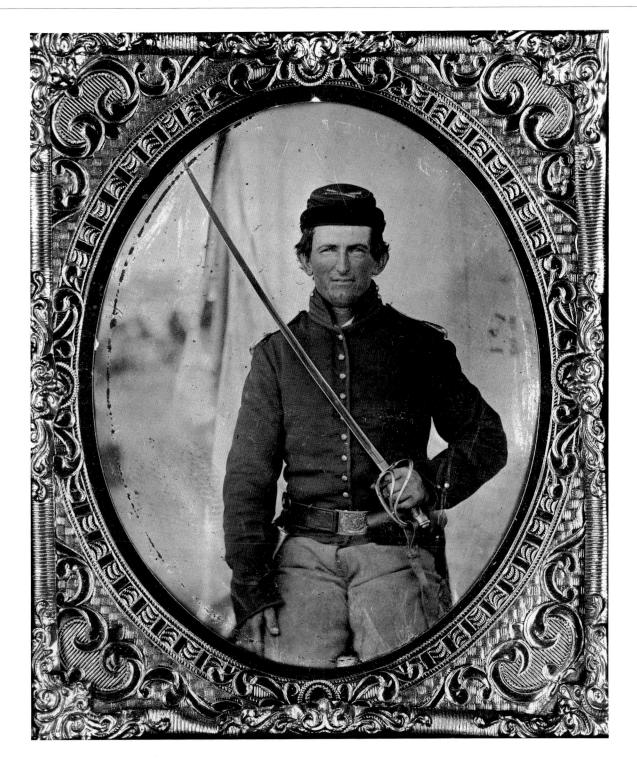

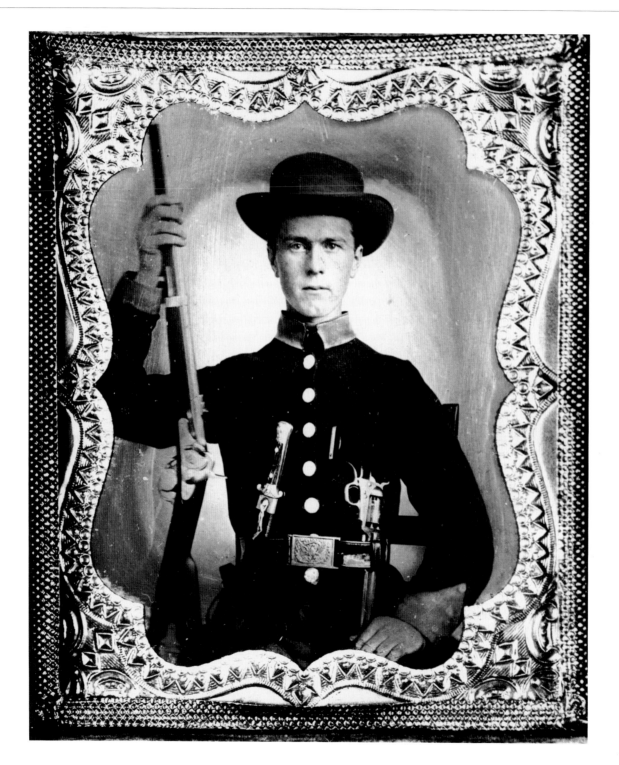

A Confederate private at the Battle of Atlanta:

We rushed forward up the steep hillsides, the seething fire from ten thousand muskets and small arms, and forty pieces of cannon hurled right into our very faces, scorching and burning our clothes and hands and faces from their rapid discharges, and piling the ground with our dead and wounded almost in heaps. It seemed that the hot flames of hell were turned loose in all their fury, while the demons of damnation were laughing in the flames like seething serpents hissing out their rage. We gave one long, loud cheer, and commenced the charge.

As we approached their lines, like a mighty inundation of the river Acheron in the infernal region, Confederate and Federal met. Officers with drawn swords met officers with drawn swords, and man to man met man to man with bayonets and loaded guns. The continued roar of battle sounded like unbottled thunder. Blood covered the ground, and the dense smoke filled our eyes, and ears, and faces. The groans of the wounded and dying rose above the thunder of battle. But the Federal lines waver, and break and fly, leaving us in possession of their breastworks and the battlefield, and I do not know how many pieces of artillery, prisoners and small arms.

Lieutenant Robert Hurt, adjutant of the 55th Tennessee, posed here with a Model 1855 rifle, side knife, and a Colt revolver, was killed at the Battle of Franklin, November 30, 1864, three months after Atlanta. The weapons are probably photographer's props, since it is unlikely that an officer would carry either a rifle or a side knife.

On February 3, 1864, Captain John B. Coleman, Company D, 60th Illinois Volunteer Infantry, petitioned for a hardship leave of absence:

> *Sir*
>
> *I most respectfully ask a leave of absence for thirty (30) days and assign the following reasons.*
>
> *I have got urgent* Business *at home that requires my immediate attention.*
>
> *When I entered the Service I was engaged in a Partnership Business and was compelled to leave it unsettled by reason of my partner being absent at the time of my enlistment. My partner is still carrying on the Business of which I am interested in the amount of Four Thousand $4,000 Dollars which he has received the benefit of—since I have been in the Service. I have used every means in my power to procure a settlement by writing, and employing an attorney. But he refuses to do anything about the settlement unless I am present. And were I to die or get killed it would leave the entire amount in his hands, where by my family could not receive a cent, if he felt disposed to prevent it as I have nothing to show that I was interested in the* Business.
>
> *I have been in the Service since the original organization of the Regiment and have never been* absent.
>
> *My P.O. address while absent would be Mount Vernon Ills*
>
> *I hope you will consider the above reasons Sufficient to grant my request.*
>
> > *I will remain*
> > *Your Obet. Servt*
> > *J. B. Coleman Capt*
> > *Comdg Co. D. 60th Ills Inft*

Coleman was granted twenty days' leave on February 6, 1864. He was killed in action at Atlanta on July 20, 1864.

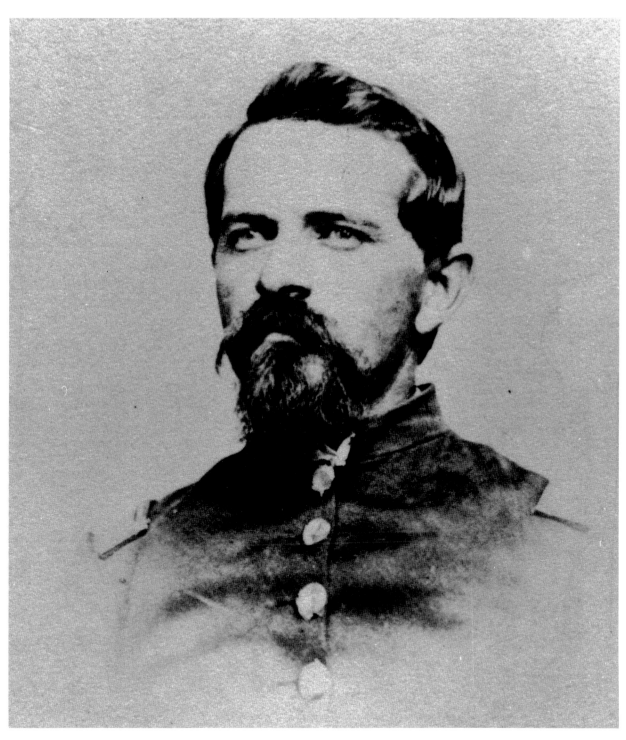

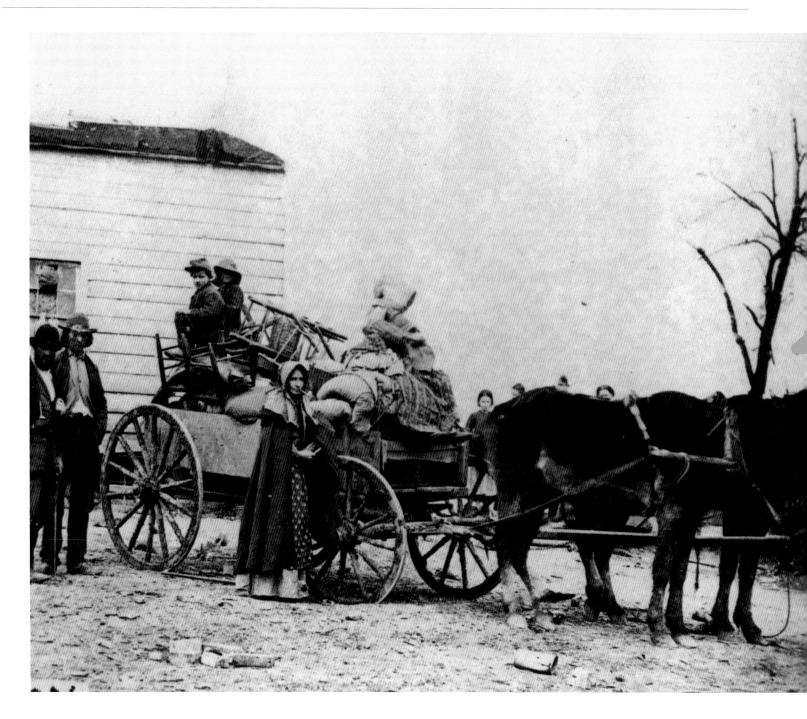

An unknown photographer captured a familiar scene in the wake of Sherman's march to the sea: a Southern refugee family. The general's aide-de-camp recorded in his diary:

As rumors of the approach of our army reached the frightened inhabitants, frantic efforts were made to conceal not only their valuable personal effects, plate, jewelry, and other rich goods, but also articles of food, such as hams, sugar, flour, etc. A large part of these supplies were carried to the neighboring swamps; but the favorite method of concealment was the burial of the treasures in the pathways and gardens adjoining the dwelling-houses. Sometimes, also, the graveyards were selected as the best place of security from the "vandal hands of the invaders."

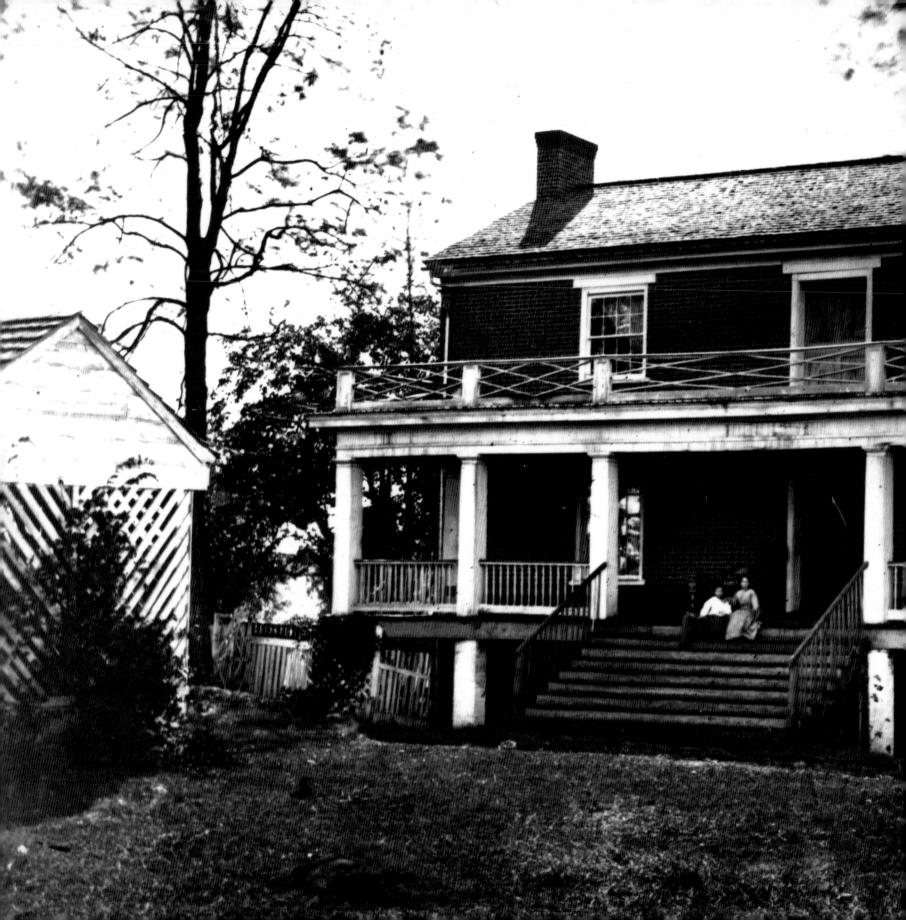

APPOMATTOX

April 8, 1865

By early April of 1865, Robert E. Lee, reduced to 35,000 starving and despondent troops, was all but surrounded by Grant's Union Army, which outnumbered him almost five to one. When Grant sent him a note under a flag of truce calling on him to surrender, Lee responded with a request for terms. Lee toyed with the notion of a breakout against Phil Sheridan's troops, who were blocking the road from his position at Appomattox Courthouse. But he finally faced the inevitable, rejecting suggestions from subordinates that his men take to the woods as guerrillas. "Though I would rather die a thousand deaths," Lee said, he sent Grant a reply on April 8, offering to surrender. Grant's terms were generous: Lee's men were free to go home, taking their horses, and the officers their horses and firearms. They would not be held accountable for their role in the war so long as they abided by the peace and obeyed the laws of their own localities.

The two men met at the house shown in the photograph, the home of Wilmer McLean (whose former house at Manassas had been hit by a Yankee shell during the war's first major battle) to sign the peace. The formal ceremony of surrender three days later was conducted with suitable dignity. When Stonewall Jackson's old brigade stepped forward to stack arms and surrender flags, the Union bugler blew a call to shift from order arms to carry arms. Thus the Union troops gave their Southern brethren the U.S. Army's salute of honor.

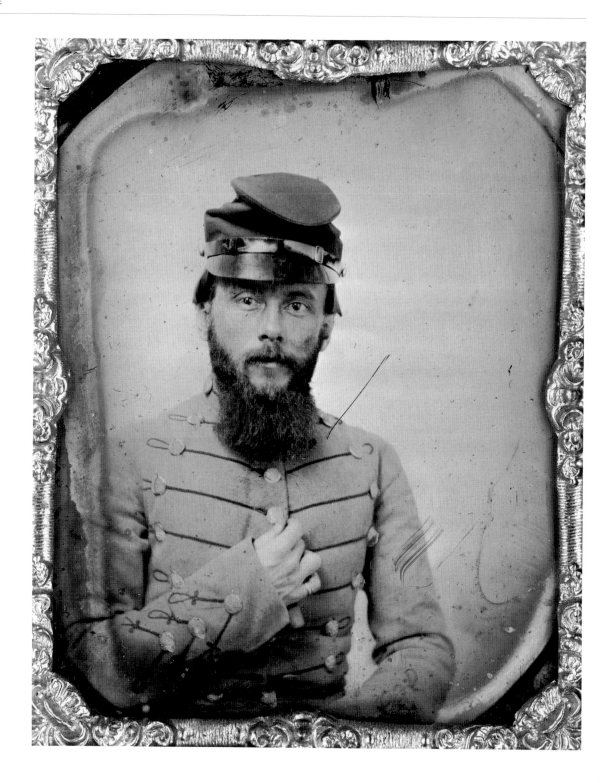

Carlton McCarthy, a history-minded private in the Army of Northern Virginia, published his recollection of Appomattox in the *Southern Historical Society Papers* in 1878:

Passing a cow-shed about this time, the squad halted to look with horror upon several dead and wounded Confederates who lay there upon the manure pile. They had suffered wounds and death upon this the last day of their country's struggle. Their wounds had received no attention, and those living were famished and burning with fever.

Lieutenant McRae, noticing a number of wagons and guns parked in a field near by, surprised at what he considered great carelessness in the immediate presence of the enemy, approached an officer on horseback and said in his usual impressive manner, "I say there, what does this mean?" The man took his hand and quietly said, "We have surrendered." "I don't believe it, sir!" replied McRae, strutting around as mad as a hornet. "You mustn't talk so, sir! You will demoralize my men!" He was soon convinced, however, by seeing Yankee cavalrymen walking their horses around as composed as though the Army of Northern Virginia had never existed.

The photograph is of Confederate Major John Roberts, whose unit is unknown.

The photograph is of an unknown Federal soldier serving with a New York regiment—most likely a cavalryman, judging from his weapons, a Smith carbine and a Remington New Army revolver—and probably no older than the Southern boy, among the war's last wounded, who speaks here:

A beautiful Southern girl, on her daily mission of love and mercy, asked a badly wounded soldier boy what she could do for him. He replied:

"I'm greatly obliged to you, but it is too late for you to do anything for me. . . . I can't live long."

"Will you not let me pray for you? I hope that I am one of the Lord's daughters, and I would like to ask Him to help you."

Looking intently into her bewitching face, he replied: "Yes, pray at once and ask the Lord to let me be His son-in-law."

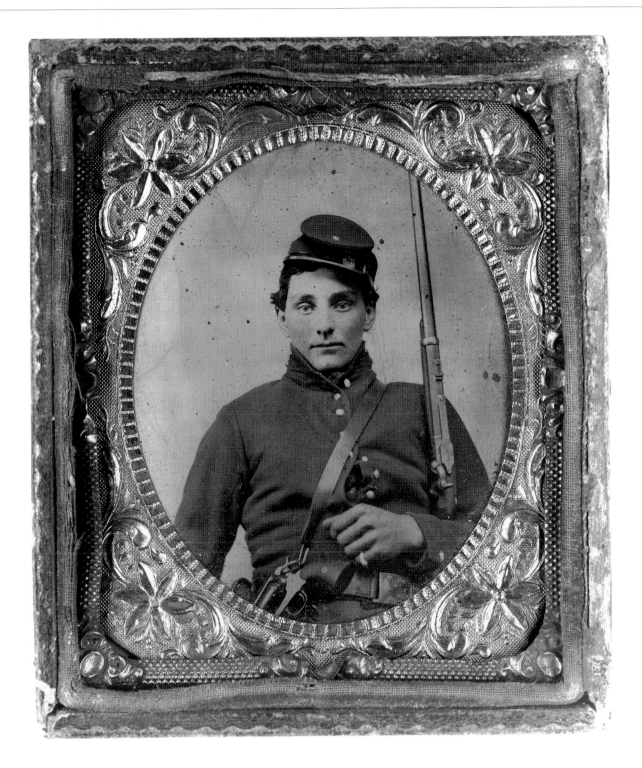

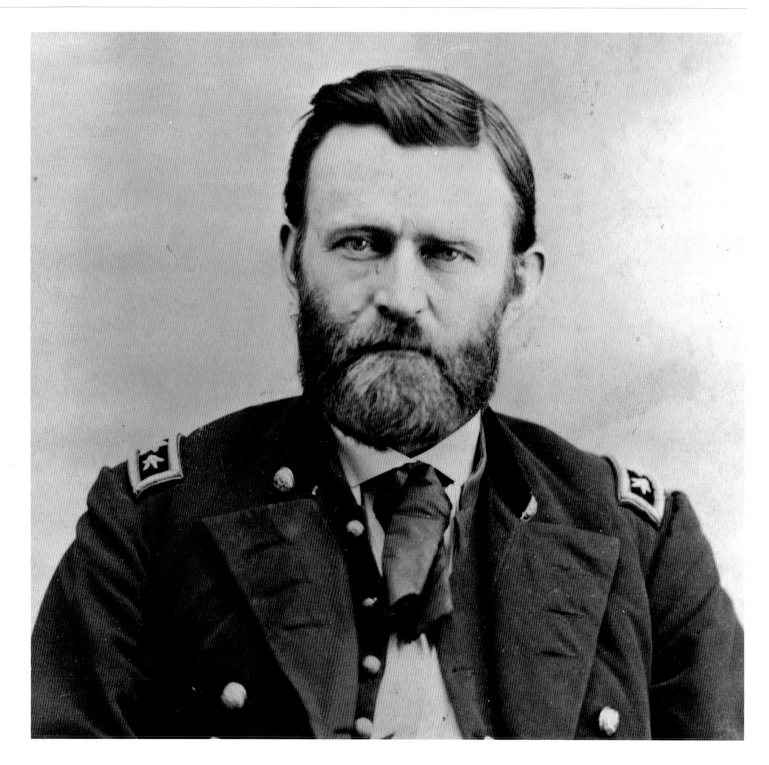

General Ulysses Simpson Grant recorded in his best-selling *Personal Memoirs*:

When I went into the house I found General Lee. We greeted each other, and after shaking hands took our seats. I had my staff with me, a good portion of whom were in the room during the whole of the interview.

What General Lee's feelings were I do not know. As he was a man of much dignity, with an impassible face . . . his feelings . . . were entirely concealed from my observation; but my own feelings . . . were sad and depressed. I felt like anything rather than rejoicing at the downfall of a foe who had fought so long and valiantly and had suffered so much. . . .

General Lee was dressed in a full uniform which was entirely new, and was wearing a sword of considerable value. . . . In my rough traveling suit . . . I must have contrasted very strangely with a man so handsomely dressed, six feet high and of faultless form. . . .

We soon fell into a conversation about old army times. . . . Our conversation grew so pleasant that I almost forgot the object of our meeting.

Headquarters, Army of Northern Virginia
April 10th, 1865

After four years of arduous service, marked by unsurpassed courage and fortitude, the Army of Northern Virginia has been compelled to yield to overwhelming numbers and resources. I need not tell the survivors of so many hard-fought battles, who have remained steadfast to the last, that I have consented to this result from no distrust of them, but, feeling that valor and devotion could accomplish nothing that could compensate for the loss that would have attended the continuation of the contest, I have determined to avoid the useless sacrifice of those whose past services have endeared them to their countrymen.

By the terms of the agreement, officers and men can return to their homes, and remain there until exchanged. You will take with you the satisfaction that proceeds from the consciousness of duty faithfully performed; and I earnestly pray that a merciful God will extend to you his blessing and protection.

With an increasing admiration for your constancy and devotion to your country, and a grateful remembrance of your kind and generous consideration of myself, I bid you an affectionate farewell.

R. E. Lee, General

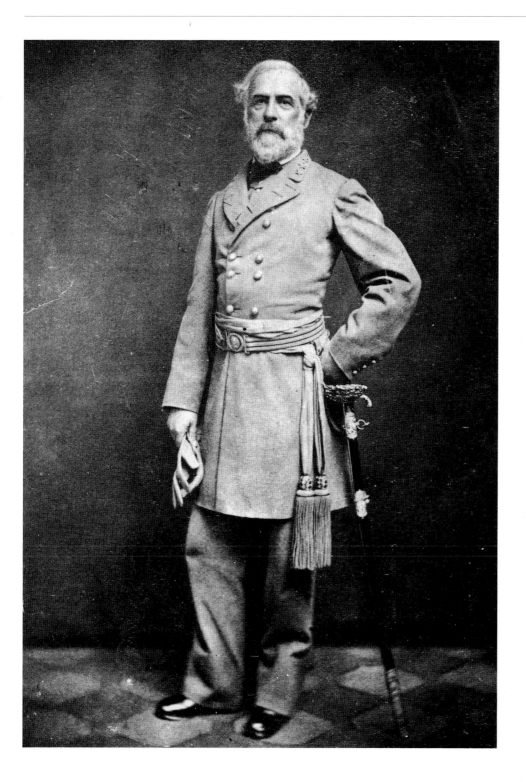

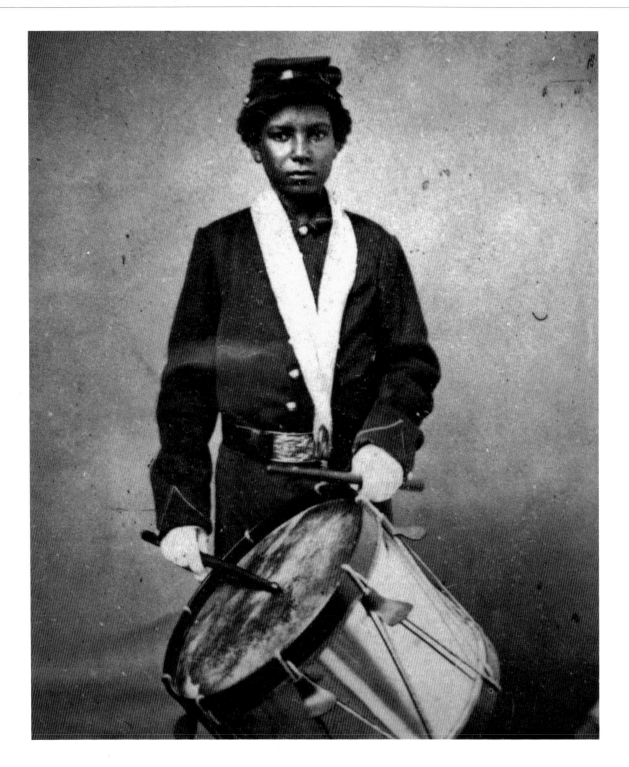

F ragment from a correspondent's report, Chickamauga:

A little waif of a drummer boy, [who had] somehow drifted up the mountain in the surge, lies there, his pale face upward, a blue spot on his breast. Muffle his drum for the poor child and his mother!

The drummer boy photographed here is known to us only as "Taylor," 78th U.S. Colored Troops, part of the "Corps d'Afrique" General Ben Butler formed in Louisiana.

TEXT SOURCES AND BIBLIOGRAPHY

Adams, F. Colburn. *The Story of a Trooper.* New York: Dick & Fitzgerald, 1865.

Annals of the War. Philadelphia: The Times Publishing Company, 1879.

Austin, J. P. *The Blue and the Gray.* Atlanta: Franklin Printing and Publishing, 1899.

Barton, William E. *The Life of Clara Barton.* Boston: Houghton, Mifflin, 1922.

Blackford, William W. *War Years with Jeb Stuart.* New York: Scribner's, 1945.

Caldwell, J. F. J. *The History of a Brigade of South Carolinians.* Philadelphia: King & Baird, 1866.

Chesnut, Mary Boykin. *A Diary from Dixie.* New York: D. Appleton, 1905.

Coffin, Charles Carleton. *My Days and Nights on the Battle-Field.* Boston: Ticknor and Fields, 1863.

Cox, Jacob D. *Atlanta.* New York: Scribner's, 1882.

Crary, Catherine S. *Dear Belle: Letters from a Cadet and Officer to His Sweetheart, 1858-1865.* Middletown, Connecticut: Wesleyan University Press, 1965.

Cumming, Kate. *A Journal of Hospital Life in the Confederate Army of Tennessee.* Louisville: John P. Morton, 1866.

De Trobriand, P. Regis. *Four Years with the Army of the Potomac.* Boston: Ticknor and Company, 1889.

Doolady, M. *Jefferson Davis and Stonewall Jackson.* Philadelphia: John E. Potter, 1866.

Doubleday, Abner. *Chancellorsville and Gettysburg.* New York: Scribner's, 1882.

Doubleday, Abner. *Reminiscences of Forts Sumter and Moultrie, 1860-1861.* New York: Harper & Brothers, 1876.

Edmonds, S. Emma E. *Nurse and Spy in the Union Army.* Hartford: W. S. Williams & Co., 1865.

Gerrish, Theodore. *Army Life: A Private's Reminiscences of the Civil War.* Portland, Maine: Hoyt, Fogg & Donham, 1883.

Goodloe, Albert Theodore. *Some Rebel Relics from the Seat of War.* Nashville: Publishing House of the Methodist Episcopal Church, South, 1893.

Gordon, John B. *Reminiscences of the Civil War.* New York: Scribner's, 1903.

Goss, Warren Lee. *Recollections of a Private.* New York: Thomas Y. Crowell, 1890.

Grant, U. S. *Personal Memoirs.* New York: Charles L. Webster, 1894.

Higginson, Thomas Wentworth. *Army Life in a Black Regiment.* 1870; reprint ed., East Lansing: Michigan State University Press, 1960.

Hill, A. F. *Our Boys: The Personal Experiences of a Soldier in the Army of the Potomac.* Philadelphia: The Keystone Publishing Co., 1890.

Howe, M. A. DeWolfe, ed. *Home Letters of General Sherman.* New York: Scribner's, 1909.

Hunter, Alexander. "A High Private's Account of the Battle of Sharpsburg," *Southern Historical Society Papers* 10, nos. 10-11 (October-November 1882): 508-509.

Lamb, Colonel William. Diary entry of November 24, 1864. Diary of Colonel William Lamb, October 24, 1864-January 14, 1865. William Lamb Papers, Manuscripts Collection, Earl Greg Swem Library, College of William and Mary.

Livermore, Mary A. *My Story of the War.* Hartford: A. D. Worthington, 1889.

Logan, John A. *The Volunteer Soldier of America.* Chicago and New York: R. S. Peale & Co., 1887.

Longstreet, James. *From Manassas to Appomattox: Memoirs of the Civil War in America.* Reprint ed., Millwood, N.Y.: Kraus Reprint, 1981.

Lusk, William Thompson. *War Letters.* Privately printed, 1911.

Luvaas, Jay, ed. *The Civil War: A Soldier's View; A Collection of Civil War Writings By Col. G. F. R. Henderson.* Chicago: University of Chicago Press, 1958.

McCarthy, Carlton. "Detailed Minutiae of Soldier Life," *Southern Historical Society Papers* 6, no. 1 (July 1878): 1-9.

McCarthy, Carlton. *Detailed Minutiae of Soldier Life in the Army of Northern Virginia 1861-1865*. Richmond: Carlton McCarthy and Co., 1882.

McPherson, James M. *The Negro's Civil War*. New York: Random House, 1965.

Menge, W. Springer, and J. August Shimrak, eds. *The Civil War Notebook of Daniel Chisholm: A Chronicle of Daily Life in the Union Army 1864-1865*. New York: Ballantine, 1989.

Moffat, George H. "War Prison Experiences," *Confederate Veteran* 13, no. 3 (March 1905): 105-10.

Nichols, George Ward. *A Soldier's Story of His Regiment*. Kennesaw, Georgia: Continental Book Company, 1961; facsimile of 1898 ed.

Nichols, George Ward. *The Story of the Great March*. New York: Harper & Brothers, 1865.

O'Ferrall, Charles T. *Forty Years of Active Service*. New York: The Neale Publishing Company, 1904.

Owen, William Miller. *In Camp and Battle with the Washington Artillery*. Boston: Ticknor and Company, 1885.

Pickett, George E. *The Heart of a Soldier*. New York: Seth Moyle, 1913.

Ray, James M. *Histories of the Several Regiments and Battalions from North Carolina in the Great War, 1861-'65*. Goldsboro, North Carolina: Nash Brothers, 1901.

Ridley, Bromfield. *Battles and Sketches of the Army of Tennessee*. Mexico, Missouri: Missouri Printing and Publishing Company, 1906.

Robertson, James I., Jr. *Soldiers Blue and Gray*. Columbia: University of South Carolina Press, 1988.

Russell, William Howard. *My Diary North and South*. Gloucester, Massachusetts: Peter Smith, 1969.

Schwartz, Gerald, ed. *A Woman Doctor's Civil War: Esther Hill Hawks' Diary*. Columbia: University of South Carolina Press, 1984.

Sears, Stephen W. *Landscape Turned Red: The Battle of Antietam*. New Haven and New York: Ticknor and Fields, 1983.

Sherman, William T. *Memoirs*. New York: D. Appleton and Co., 1875.

Stewart, A. M. *Camp, March, and Battle-Field*. Philadelphia: Jas. B. Rodgers, 1865.

Stiles, Robert. *Four Years Under Marse Robert*. New York and Washington: Neale, 1903.

Swanberg, W. A. *First Blood: The Story of Fort Sumter*. New York: Scribner's, 1957.

Swanberg, W. A. *Sickles the Incredible*. New York: Scribner's, 1956.

Von Borcke, Heros. *Memoirs of the Confederate War for Independence*. New York: Peter Smith, 1938; facsimile of 1866 edition.

Watkins, Samuel R. *"Co. Aytch."* Jackson, Tennessee: McCowat-Mercer Press, 1952.

Wheeler, Richard. *Sword Over Richmond: An Eyewitness History of McClellan's Peninsula Campaign*. New York: Harper and Row, 1968.

Wheeler, Richard. *Voices of the Civil War*. New York: Thomas Y. Crowell, 1976.

Whitman, Walt. *Complete Poems and Prose of Walt Whitman, 1855-1888*. Philadelphia, 1888-89.

Williams, Blanche. *Clara Barton: Daughter of Destiny*. Philadelphia: J. B. Lippincott, 1941.

Worsham, John H. *One of Jackson's Foot Cavalry*. New York: Neale Publishing Company, 1912.

Wright, Charles. *A Corporal's Story*. Philadelphia: James Beale, 1887.

Young, Jesse Bowman. *What a Boy Saw in the Army*. New York: Hunt & Eaton, 1894.

INDEX